You don't need a title to start leading.

When Everyone Leads:
How Tough Challenges Get Seen and Solved

By Ed O'Malley & Julia Fabris McBride

Table of Contents

Redefining Leadership

A 10-Point Manifesto

1.

Tough challenges are all around us.

A nonprofit isn't sustainable.

A small business barely stays profitable after the founder moves on.

A school struggles to help a city's most vulnerable children thrive academically.

A nation grows more divided.

Those challenges appear in our professional lives, in our communities, and in our families. They polarize and perplex us. They can seem unsolvable, unreachable, and beyond our ability to grasp what needs to be done.

Our toughest challenges baffle us. We can work on them for days, weeks, or even years and still not see progress.

Passion for progress isn't the same as progress.

Often, we are stuck.

Progress requires leadership.

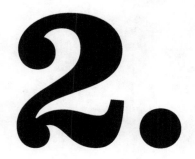

Most think leadership is a position. (It's not.)

Most think leadership is meant for the few. (Wrong again.)

When people say, "Let's ask leadership about this," they mean let's ask the people in charge. When they say, "The company has a new leader," they mean there is a new CEO.

If someone sends you to a leadership program, they are probably preparing you to be a manager, or a manager of managers. If they give you a leadership coach, chances are they think you are ready for even more direct reports, for an even more important spot in the hierarchy.

3.

Leadership _isn't_ ...

Authority
Being the boss
Vision
Charisma
A servant's heart
An inspirational speech

Leadership _could_ involve these things, and many more, but it isn't literally these things.

4.

Imagine if people thought about practicing leadership or exercising leadership, rather than "being a leader."

We don't like the word *leader*. We know people use it all the time, but it doesn't seem helpful. A lot of times, so called *leaders* don't lead.

If leadership is a practice, anyone can do it. Some might do it more effectively than others, but everyone *can* do it. And everyone *can* get better at it.

A whole lot more becomes possible if we see leadership through this appreciative and inclusive lens.

5.

Plenty of people in important positions never exercise leadership.

The world is full of bad and mediocre bosses, coaches, presidents, and CEOs.

Leadership position and *leadership team* are outdated terms from a model that no longer works. The "leadership as a position" model is collapsing. The world is moving too fast. The pace of change is too unforgiving. Organizations that expect people at the top to do all the leading won't thrive. At best they'll survive.

The pace of change makes it too hard for the relatively few people who head up teams, committees, companies, agencies, cities, and countries to shoulder all the leadership necessary for success. They lack sufficient perspective and knowledge to solve multifaceted problems in an increasingly diverse society.

And the traditional "leadership as authority" model lets the rest of us off the hook. We tell ourselves that since we aren't in charge, we aren't responsible for what's wrong. We say it's the CEO's fault or the governor's fault or the pastor's fault. We leave the creativity, risk, and responsibility for change to someone else, someone higher on the org chart.

6.

So, most of us don't lead.

Everyone is calculating what their boss, board of directors, teacher, principal, manager, voters, and friends expect of them. Then they do those things and hope to meet those expectations.

Followership keeps other people happy and you out of trouble. A CEO keeps her board of directors feeling secure and in control. A manager reads his job description and follows it exactly.

A teacher follows the principal. The principal follows the superintendent. The superintendent follows the school board. The school board follows the voters.

Followership plays out most clearly among politicians. Politicians are lagging indicators of what's going on in society. Change rarely starts with them. A politician anticipates what their voters want and then follows the crowd that put them in office.

Get good at following and people will call you a success! You'll get promoted. You'll be called a team player. Keep it up and you'll get promoted again and again. Eventually they will make you a "leader." Never mind that all you've done is follow expectations set out for you.

Leadership is an activity, not a position or authority.

It is an activity available to all of us.

Leadership emerged in 1955 when Rosa Parks refused to give up her seat on the bus. Leadership emerges whenever a new employee asks a question no one wants to answer.

Kids are told, *"Anyone can be a leader!"* They see images of people of all genders, races, and abilities sitting behind a big desk, taking an oath of office, or managing an emergency. Yes, every kid needs to know they can work hard and achieve great things.

But kids (and adults) must also understand that leadership and position are two different things. Kids (and adults) need to know they can exercise leadership whether they have a formal position or not.

Leadership has nothing to do with role. It has everything to do with seeing and seizing moments to help a group move forward.

8.

If anyone can lead, then everyone can lead.

When everyone leads, amazing things happen. Tough problems become simpler. Big aspirations become reachable.

When everyone leads, organizations are productive, not just busy. People are purposeful, not just going through the motions.

When everyone leads, emotion gets channeled into teamwork.

When everyone leads, it's not up to the boss to ask all the right questions. People inspire one another to stay focused on what's most important.

When everyone leads, frustration, gossip, and office politics give way to engagement, productivity, and a shared sense of accomplishment.

Solutions to big, important challenges emerge. People make progress together.

When authorities—the folks with the top jobs—empower others to lead, their own jobs get easier. When everyone else—the folks not in authority—starts leading, their work becomes more rewarding.

Organizations, companies, and communities are more successful when everyone leads.

9.

Leadership is risky.

A moment that could benefit from our leadership comes right at us, but we let it go. We don't take the swing. We don't seize it because we are afraid of making a mistake. We would rather blame someone else for a problem than do something about it ourselves. Because once we try something, once we see and seize our moment, there is no turning back.

Leadership is risky because once you intervene, you have a stake in the outcome and you can't be sure what will happen next.

10.

And it's not leadership if it's not about our most important challenges.

Every organization, company, or community has concernsand unmet aspirations. Leadership is about the biggest of these. Leadership is an activity designed to make progress on the things that concern us the most, those that we most aspire to achieve.

Leadership is mobilizing people to make progress on the most important challenges. And it's rare.

More than fifteen years ago, a foundation committed tens of millions of dollars to build leadership capacity in our part of the world. The board of that foundation came to a profound conclusion:

The quality and quantity of leadership is a key determinant to prosperity, health, and success for organizations and communities.

We launched the Kansas Leadership Center (KLC) in 2007. Ed's background was in government and politics. Julia was an actor turned leadership coach. We guide this training, engagement, and research center, overseeing an experiment unlike any in the world. Nowhere else is a leadership development effort as well-financed and as focused on leadership for everyone in communities, organizations, and companies.

After 15 years, over 15,000 participants, and partnerships throughout our state but also around the world, our research and experience support a powerful promise:

When Everyone Leads, We Make Progress on Our Most Important Challenges

You can see exactly that in our programs. There's a firefighter, teacher, banker, pastor, and politician in one small group. Another has a construction worker, nurse, university president, social worker, and a business owner. Yet another has a school principal, nonprofit volunteer, corporate middle manager, an engineer, and a game warden.

Some are early in their careers. Others are seasoned with decades of experience. They come from organizations big and small, from urban and rural communities, and from all sectors. Some are liberal. Others are conservative.

Dozens come from each organization. Hundreds learn, practice, and engage together. Thousands every year.

Their experience disrupts how they think about leadership, what leadership is, and who it is for. They embrace our leadership model and use it to create profound change in their organizations, companies, and communities.

The KLC experience is countercultural. It runs against the grain. It upends norms. Still, people from all walks of life engage with us. They learn a very different way of exercising leadership.

They are on a journey. You are too. Welcome.

Let These Principles Guide Your Way

Principle #1:
Leadership is an activity, not a position.

Leadership and authority are two different things. *Leadership* is mobilizing others to solve their most important challenges. *Authority* is more like management. Having good people in authority positions is absolutely necessary to keep things functioning at a high level, but authority alone is not sufficient to make progress on the things that matter most.

Principle #2:
Anyone can lead, anytime, anywhere.

If we want to solve our most important challenges, more people need to embrace the idea that everyone can lead. When it comes to our toughest challenges, we all have a part to play. Lots of people need to contribute time and energy. Saying "yes" to the idea that anyone can see and seize their moment to lead means risking your own comfort for the sake of progress on something that matters.

Principle #3:
Leadership starts with you and must engage others.

Some things an expert can fix or the boss can order done. But as a culture, we've fallen into the bad habit of waiting for others to lead. When you embrace this principle, the waiting is over. Action is yours to take and the time is now. No matter your position, age, or level of experience, you can do something to mobilize others to make progress on an important leadership challenge. The goal of taking action is not to fix things yourself but to engage other people.

Principle #4:
Leadership is risky.

If you've ever attempted to get people to work together on a difficult challenge, you know that leadership is risky. We want to drive home this principle as both a warning and encouragement. Even as you do everything you can to energize others to solve a big challenge, pay attention and build your skill at minimizing risks.

Principle #5:
Leadership is about our toughest challenges.

You have to care about something really important—an aspiration or a big concern. Without a clear sense of purpose nothing is going to change. It's not leadership if it's not about those tough challenges.

Part One

Identify The Gap

Leadership always starts with dissatisfaction. No one exercises leadership unless they are unhappy with the current reality. We only do it when we see something lacking and care enough to change it. When we sense things could be better for those we care about, we motivate ourselves to see and seize our moments to lead.

Most groups don't do a good job of assessing their current reality. Too often we tell ourselves everything is fine, that we are headed in the right direction. We convince ourselves we are on track to meet our mission. We don't pause to examine big concerns or articulate bold aspirations. Compelling reasons to exercise leadership remain unspoken. Concerns and aspirations that could fuel progress go unexplored.

Thousands of people have come through our leadership and civic engagement programs over the last 15 years. For them, *The Gap* is shorthand for their most important challenges. It's the distance between their current reality and their aspirations.

- A school aspires to be a viable choice for families throughout the city, but right now only people who can't afford to move elsewhere attend.

- A company aspires to dominate the market with their product, but it struggles for a foothold.

- A rural community aspires to grow its economy by supporting entrepreneurs, but it hasn't had a successful start-up in years.

Like most groups, people from that school, company, and community see a big gap between their current reality and the way they want things to be. But the old way of thinking about leadership—that it's about an authority figure out in front, shepherding followers toward a predetermined goal—lets them down. It places responsibility for seeing The Gap at the very top of the hierarchy. It sidelines countless people and creative ideas for change.

Groups that want to solve their toughest challenges need everyone, at all levels, to understand:

1. **Start with seeing The Gap.** There are lots of reasons to avoid looking at The Gap. Those who exercise leadership do it anyway.

2. **The Gap starts with concerns.** Don't avoid naming the tough stuff. You can't change something you won't acknowledge.

3. **The Gap is fueled by aspirations.** Dreams for the future bring with them the courage and energy to exercise leadership.

4. **Everyone can see The Gap.** Ask powerful questions to generate conversation about your toughest challenges and inspire everyone to lead.

5. **The Gap is full of adaptive challenges and technical problems.** If you want to make more progress, you need to know the difference between the two.

2
Seeing The Gap

Don't underestimate how hard it is to face our current reality. And as difficult as it is to talk frankly about concerns, it may be even harder to express dreams for the future that are bold enough to fuel positive change. But to exercise leadership, we have to take that leap. We have to look for The Gap. It's only when we are brave enough to acknowledge big concerns and talk about bold aspirations that we see our toughest challenges for what they are.

Most of the time we avoid turning attention to The Gap, and for plenty of understandable reasons:

- **The tyranny of the present.** We are consumed by what is right in front of us. Colleagues put meetings on our calendar. Kids need rides to soccer practice. The lawn needs mowing. That report was due to the boss yesterday.

- **Rewards for being busy, not productive.** We are more often rewarded for being busy than productive. Many organizations bestow invisible badges of honor on those who work 60 hours per week. The fact that few of those hours were devoted to what's most important often seems irrelevant.

"I hate to be the one to bring up the planet-killing, cosmic void in the room, but..."

- **Aversion to thinking about anything negative.** It is hard to see The Gap if we always look at the bright side. If your culture is built around celebration, good news, wins, successes, strengths, and gratitude (all great things to focus on!) it could be difficult, at first, to get people talking about what's not working. They may need permission to ponder unrealized aspirations.

- **The illusion of agreement.** When we contemplate The Gap we elevate conflicting perspectives that most of us prefer not to see. Economist Daniel Kahneman refers to this human tendency to avoid disagreeing with colleagues as "the illusion of agreement." His research with insurance underwriters shows that over time, individuals learnto conform their judgments rather than experience the discomfort of disagreement.

- **Focusing on The Gap will require ... focus!** Avoiding The Gap allows everyone to stay busy doing their thing, going in their own direction, doing what they feel comfortable doing. Progress requires shaking things up. Most of us would rather stay comfortable.

- **We sense (correctly) that once we acknowledge The Gap, we'll have hard choices to make.** Exercising leadership is almost always about doing less rather than more. It's about saying "no" to 99 things so you can say one huge "yes" to an important challenge.

In the long-term, you will be rewarded for exercising leadership on your group's toughest challenges. But in the short-term, you may be criticized or even vilified. There are lots of reasons to avoid looking at The Gap. Those who exercise leadership do it anyway.

Once The Gap between concerns and aspirations becomes clear, we see that progress will require us to let some things go. Changing how we operate is hard, especially if it disappoints people we seek to please. Most of us would rather keep doing what we're doing and keep most stakeholders moderately appeased than make difficult choices to focus our efforts on what matters most.

Everyone Needs to Look at The Gap

Important things happen when enough people look at The Gap. We all start operating at a different level. Groups generate new energy. No matter our position, when we acknowledge The Gap, we immediately see that achieving our greatest aspirations takes collective work and individuals stretching outside their comfort zones. As people up and down the organizational chart talk about their biggest concerns and greatest aspirations, a message permeates the organization: Moments are there for the seizing. We need leadership from the many, not the few.

How Do You See The Gap?

Seeing The Gap takes the courage to focus on what's not going well. The process isn't difficult. Answer these questions and you'll see The Gap:

1. When you think about the future (of your company, your organization, your team, your community, or your family) what concerns you *the most*?

2. When you think about the future (of that same group of people) what is your *greatest* aspiration?

3. What makes it hard to close The Gap between those concerns and aspirations?

Once you've answered these questions, you'll want to ask them of others, too. Chapter 5 has a short guide for facilitating a team conversation about The Gap.

Leadership starts with everyone seeing The Gap between their current reality and greatest aspirations.

MAKING IT REAL

Dear Ed and Julia,

I serve as CEO of a large company in our city and also serve as the spokesperson for our industry. I am the board chair for our local chamber of commerce and sit on numerous other nonprofit boards. I served two terms as a city commissioner and am regularly asked to run for mayor. Are you saying I'm not a leader?

—Bob the CEO

Dear Bob,

Plenty of people cycle in and out of key roles with The Gap remaining the same as before. Leadership is mobilizing people to close The Gap. It is not simply holding authority.

We prefer to talk about exercising leadership, rather than labeling people "leader" or "not leader." You haven't given us enough information to know whether you exercise leadership. Given your civic and professional involvement, you must have deep passion and commitment for service. The key question is whether your community, company, and those nonprofits have made progress. Are the concernsthe same as before? Are the aspirations the same too?

Your positions of authority afford you unique opportunities to exercise leadership. And, yet, you'll likely need to help others see and seize their moments to exercise leadership too. You might consider using your roles to help others see The Gap. Once they do, we bet leadership will start emerging from many people and places. Think about what your company and your community can accomplish when everyone leads!

3
The Gap Starts With Concerns

It's possible to be a glass half-full person and also understand leadership requires dissatisfaction with the current reality. Dissatisfaction that fuels leadership isn't about little stuff. (It's not complaints about colleagues not picking up after themselves in the break room or frustrations about a partner not doing their fair share of the work.)

Dissatisfaction that fuels leadership is future oriented and related to big, important things that concern us *the most:*

- When a 20-something Latina thinks about the future of the large regional bank where she works, she's most concerned about the lack of diversity in senior positions.

- When a longtime member of a local school board thinks about the future of the school district, he's most concerned about the number of students below grade level in reading and math. (It's the same concern that led him to run for the school board 12 years ago.)

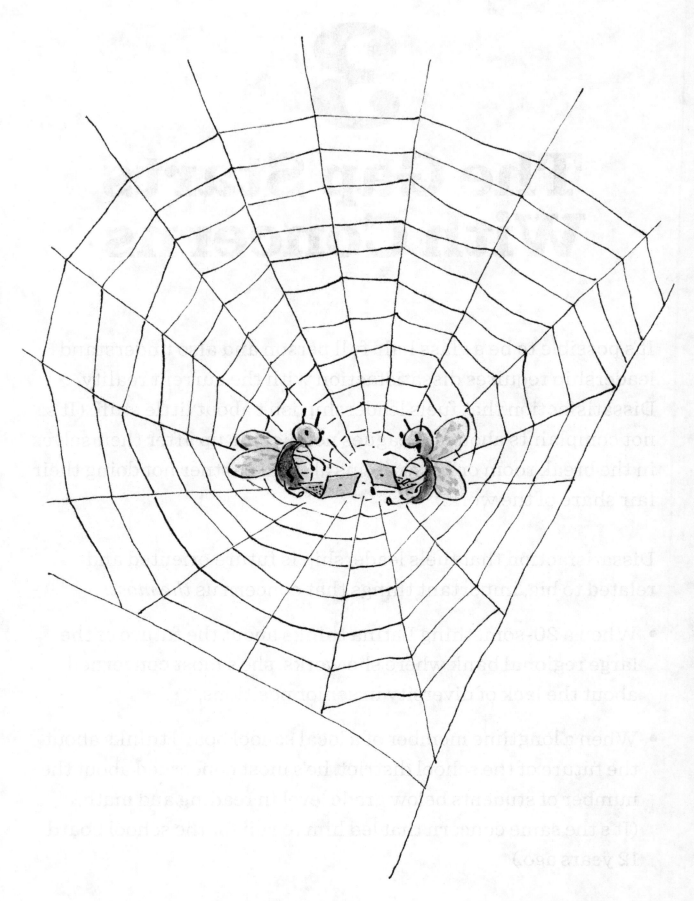

"We're here because we want to be, not because we are 'stuck'."

- When a middle manager in a large global company thinks about the future, they're most concerned about the lack of shared purpose that has plagued the team for years.

- When a rabbi thinks about the future of her synagogue, she's most concerned about antisemitism at the nearby university, something she began noticing a decade ago.

- When a college freshman thinks about the future of his family, he's most concerned about his parents' failing health due to poor diet and a sedentary lifestyle.

Those who exercise leadership channel their frustration with the current reality into thoughts about progress. They see where things are today and where they want them to be someday.

They feel deeply discontented with the status quo and usethat discontent to open their hearts to change. Their biggest concerns fire them up to work toward a better future for themselves and those they care about.

Tough Issues Emerge When People Talk About the Future

Tough issues are revealed when we ask people to think about *the future* and what concerns them the most. Issues emerge that need more leadership.

Ask others about their biggest concerns, and you'll hear about:

- **Long-standing issues.** These things didn't pop up last week.

- **Issues that can't be blamed on one person or department.** These issues permeate the system. They are in the culture. Firing one person or restructuring one team won't fix them.

- **Issues with complicated histories.** People usually don't agree about why or how the issues emerged.

- **Issues with no clear way forward.** Likewise, people usually don't agree about the best steps to take to solve the underlying problems.

If you want to improve quality of life in a community, your biggest concerns might be "the growing divide between the haves and have-nots" or "our inability to diversifyour economy." If you're thinking about an organization or company, answers might be "working in silos" or "unsustainable income streams." For a department or team, answers might be "our inability to complete projects on time" or "the rift between customer-facing and behind-the-scenes staff."

It's likely good people have been working on these issues for a long time, but if these are the things that concern you the most, then surely more is needed. These issues need leadership that is more provocative and inclusive. These concerns need leadership from the many, not the few.

Exploring our biggest concerns is just half of The Gap. It's the pragmatic part. You have to identify what's not working. Balancing pragmatism with healthy idealism is the subject of the next chapter.

MAKING IT REAL

Dear Ed and Julia,

I'm a partner in a small consulting business working with clients across the country and a few outside the states. We have 14 full-time staff members, and what concerns me the most when I think about the future is how exhausted we are all the time! New work keeps coming in, which lets us hire more people to help handle the new work. But, we seem to be on a treadmill that goes faster and faster. Adding new employees helps in the short run, but it puts pressure on us to sell more work in the long run. How do we focus attention and leadership? And, what exactly should we focus it on? Help, please!

—Exhausted Evelynn

Evelynn,

What concerns you the most is a business model that only works if everyone is exhausted. We bet you worry about sustainability. We would if we were in your shoes.

Perhaps your leadership challenge is to reduce time focusedon managing the current activities and increase time spent on building a new business model? It's the difference between, for example, spending every available hour trying to find the perfect client management system and dedicating that time to imagining alternative operating structures.

It doesn't seem to us that the exercise of leadership here is about working harder to manage the existing business model. Leadership in this situation is mobilizing your team to slowly shift to a new business model. We imagine that might sound hard, especially because you've created a business model that keeps winning new business!

You know what concerns you the most. That's the firststep in defining your Gap. You've focused your leadership where it's needed most.

4

The Gap Is Fueled by Aspirations

Leadership may start with dissatisfaction, but it's our aspirations that keep us in the game. No one exercises leadership without a clear picture of what they want to create or who they long to serve. Leadership is not organizing the status quo slightly more efficiently. Leadership helps a group move closer to its greatest aspirations for a new reality.

A sports team aspires to win championships. A school aspires to have all students thriving by graduation. A company aspires to lead the market. A community aspires to leverage diversity to create strength and opportunity for all.

Ed serves as board chair for the local Boys & Girls Club. The organization's greatest aspiration is access to the club for every kid in need. No one is satisfied with the current reality because right now some kids don't know about the club. Some can't afford it. Other kids don't have a club in their neighborhood. Clarity about their aspiration is pushing the organization in new directions. No longer can staff be satisfied with efficiently running a couple of club sites. The aspiration to provide access for every kid in need provides focus and inspiration.

Reaching Big Aspirations Requires the Many, Not the Few

A sports team can't win a championship with just one phenomenal player. Success requires each team member to do their part. A superstar might get most of the attention and headlines, but without every teammate leading and influencing one another, championships will be elusive.

As an actor and playwright, Julia worked with a couple of directors who were creative geniuses. But theatrical genius is useless by itself. These directors needed actors and playwrights to contribute ideas and take artistic risks. And without designers and technicians bringing their imaginations and unique perspectives, those directors would just be dreamers. Instead, thanks to collaboration by many, their companies gleaned critical acclaim. The genius directors, along with a handful of the other artists, gained national recognition. Their success was the result of everyone in all roles, giving their creative best.

Likewise, your team or organization won't reach its biggest aspirations if only one person (the top authority or the one with the most expertise) tries to lead.

Our research shows that closing The Gap takes leadership from the many, not the few. For instance, when a global high-tech company invested in leadership development for employees throughout its business units, the results were deeper diagnosis and more collaboration. Real progress on the toughest challenges facing your company or community requires more people looking at The Gap, voicing concerns and aspirations, balancing pragmatism and idealism. Progress on our most important challenges happens when enough people have skill and patience to navigate The Gap.

Aspirations Inspire Leadership

When we encourage you to talk about aspirations we don't mean overly facilitated efforts that yield watered-down "vision statements" designed not to upset anyone. These consensusdriven statements might satisfy expectations of certain factions or authorities, but they don't inspire people.

Aspirations come from our lived experience and our hopes for those we care about most. They motivate us to get up in the morning, come to work, and make things better.

- A curriculum and instruction coach cares deeply about the high-risk students in her large urban school district. Her greatest aspiration is for every child in the district to become a reader.

- A community health director cares most about the community members who depend on his organization's health clinics. His greatest aspiration is for his team to have the skills and optimism to help those clients navigate the public health system.

- A law firm partner is concerned that poor communication is demoralizing staff and leading to mistakes that impact clients. They aspire to provide the highest level of service.

What Makes It Hard to Focus on Our Greatest Aspirations?

- **We assume we need uniformity about what those aspirations should be.** We don't. The important thing is that enough people in your organization are thinking about change and positive impact. Those aspirations don't need to align perfectly.

- **Finding common ground takes time.** Although we don't always need to come to precise agreement, we do need to find some common ground. We need multiple people looking at a similar gap from diverse perspectives. Getting everyone heading in the same direction, differently, takes patience and curiosity.

- **It's important, not urgent.** Creating shared understanding among a team, group, company, or organization about our greatest aspirations is an exercise of leadership. Steven Covey described that type of work as important, not urgent. (Read his *The 7 Habits of Highly Effective People* for more.)

- **We'd rather get a respectable B– than go for an A+ and fall short.** Naming our greatest aspiration has risk built into it. If we don't name it, we can't fail to achieve it.

- **Some gaps will never be completely closed.** Many of us shrink back from naming our deepest aspirations because The Gap between where we are and where we want to be is so big and the problem so entrenched. With the toughest problems facing our communities, the best we can hope for in a lifetime is significant progress.

Big, bold aspirations are worth the effort and the risk of disappointment. Aspirations inspire and motivate. They open up opportunities and make it possible for everyone to lead. People intuitively understand that big, bold aspirations can't be achieved by just a few people. The combination of major concerns and bold aspirations is like a powerful magnet, energizing everyone's leadership in a common direction.

MAKING IT REAL

Dear Ed and Julia,

What if my colleagues can't agree on the greatest aspiration for our organization? I'm nervous about exploring aspirations with our team because I know there are unspoken differences of opinion about the current direction. I'm on the senior team of a large foundation. Since the summer of 2020, with the protests around the nation and world related to the murder of George Floyd, our organization has been pivoting to do much more to elevate issues of race and racism. I'm afraid the aspirations of some of my colleagues might be too provocative for their coworkers. And yet, I feel it's important to clarify our most important leadership opportunities. Any advice?

—Francis from the Foundation

Great question, Francis! The point of discussing aspirations isn't to gain group consensus. It's not a group visioning exercise or a replacement for a proper strategic plan. The purpose isn't to solidify behind just one leadership challenge or orienting purpose. Discussing aspirations helps people see The Gap between their current reality and desired future. Next you can explore what you each can do to close those gaps. Asking about big aspirations guides them to explore what leadership, from them and others, needs to look like in your organization.

One last thought: You mentioned "unspoken differences." Look for moments when you can encourage others (and yourself!) to give voice to those unspokens. Your organization's success is directly related to your team's ability to make the unspoken spoken. Harmony isn't the lack of dissonance but using dissonance to create something powerful and beautiful. A senior team with unspoken differences isn't in harmony. It's off-key. And that's probably obvious to anyone who's listening.

5
Everyone Can See The Gap

There's more to share about leadership on our most important challenges, but we can't resist giving a little advice early in the book. Use the three questions in this chapter with colleagues to explore The Gap in your organization, company, or community.

We've used these questions to help thousands of organizations and teams clarify The Gap between their current reality and their greatest aspirations. We use this tool regularly ourselves to keep our own organizations on track.

Do this exercise and you'll reveal issues that need more leadership from you and from others.

Set the Stage

Here's how to set the stage for a powerful and productive conversation about your Gap:

1. Choose the scope before you ask the questions of your team. Make sure everyone knows, for instance, whether the focus is on the future of the team, the department, or the whole organization.

2. Set aside at least 60 minutes to facilitate the conversation with your group.

3. Have a way to track responses for everyone to see (i.e., flip chart, whiteboard, document projected digitally, etc.).

4. Encourage people to set aside mobile phones and laptops.

5. Include time for individual reflection (for instance, after you pose each question).

6. If your group is more than six or eight people, provide them with time to discuss in pairs before they share with the larger group.

If you are the facilitator:

• Stay relaxed and present to whatever emerges.

• Make time and space for people to respond.

- Remind people repeatedly that there are no wrong answers to the questions.

- Don't work toward consensus.

- Don't push the discussion in your preferred direction. Just let it happen.

Facilitate the Three Questions

Question One: When you think about the future of _____ (your company, your team, your community, or your family) what concerns you *the most*?

- *The most* are the critical words in the question. They prevent a laundry list of concerns, frustrations, and annoyances. These words force a prioritization. "The most" is the phrase that gives this question power.

- Framing the question around the future expands thinking. People get beyond the day-to-day, focusing their minds on the big picture.

Question Two: When you think about the future of _____ (your company, your team, your community, or your family), what is your *greatest* aspiration?

- The word *greatest* primes people to think big and focuses attention on the things that matter most and that they most aspire to achieve.

- Notice the emphasis on the future. Orienting people to their desired future clarifies the organization's challenges and opportunities.

- Feel free to flip questions one and two if you think starting with aspirations will work better for your group.

Question Three: What makes it hard to close The Gap between those concerns and aspirations?

- This question should get more time than either of the first two. Answers to this question describe The Gap. Talking about concerns and aspirations (questions one and two) may not be unusual for your group, but for most people, this third question is unique and illuminating.

- The issues people talk about when they answer this question are mitigated by effective leadership.

- Encourage people to name the hard stuff. Reassure them that they don't need to know how to solve anything right now. For the purposes of this activity, naming is the important thing.

- Invite people to talk about fears and feelings that make it hard to exercise leadership in The Gap.

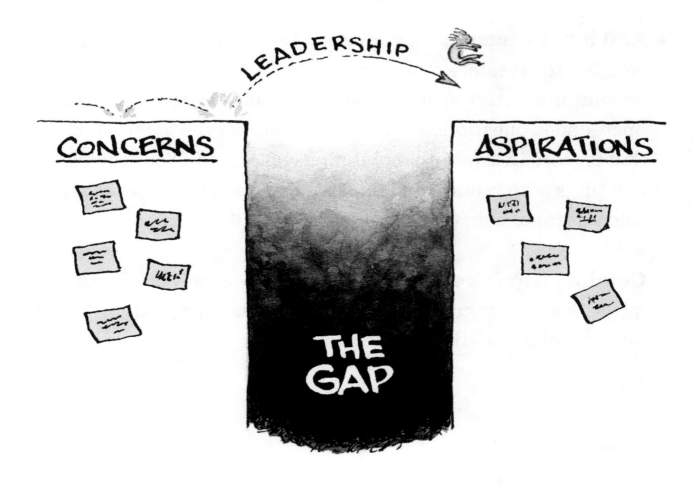

When and Where to Ask the Three Questions

We've used these questions in retreats with formal agendas, flip charts, snacks, and so on. But there are less intense ways to use the questions to illuminate The Gap and focus your leadership and the leadership of others. Here are just a few ways to get started:

- **Take a personal listening tour.** You don't need a fancy, official listening tour or offsite retreat sanctioned by the organization. Just start asking people the questions and take note of their answers. They'll point you (and themselves) in the direction of the things that need more leadership.

- **Add it to an agenda.** If you control a meeting agenda (for your board, a team, a department, etc.), add the questions to an upcoming meeting agenda. You'll be surprised how big-picture, open-ended questions stimulate a different type of meeting that is more in line with mobilizing leadership. (Your typical meetings with reports and updates may be necessary but are seldom transformative.)

- **Conduct a quick e-survey.** Create an e-survey asking the questions of your group. Then spend ample time studying their answers and drawing out themes.

MAKING IT REAL

> **Dear Ed and Julia,**
>
> **I'd love to get my team to talk about what makes progress difficult in our Gap, but I'm worried that it's going to become a complaint-fest. Does that happen? Advice appreciated!**
>
> **—Hesitating Henry**

Dear Henry,

Invite people to develop the courage to hold two things at once: what is not working and what is possible. Trust them, and hold steady yourself. Conversations like this are countercultural in most organizations. People are often afraid to look at the negative because they don't think they have the capacity to make things better. You do!

6
Adaptive Challenges and Technical Problems

The last few decades have introduced several ways to name and think about our toughest problems. But the most useful and powerful paradigm comes from Ron Heifetz and Marty Linsky and their books *The Practice of Adaptive Leadership* (also with Alexander Grashow) and *Leadership on the Line*. Heifetz and Linsky are close friends to our organizations. They continue to inspire our teaching methods and many of the ideas in our books and programs.

Ed started spending time with Heifetz and Linsky as he wrapped up a listening tour of our state asking all kinds of people about their concerns and aspirations and what makes progress difficult. Ed realized the adaptive challenge framework, developed by Heifetz and Linsky at Harvard Kennedy School, was a clear and powerful way of defining the entrenched problems people shared during the tour.

What Makes It Hard to Close The Gap?

Over the years we have asked thousands of people to think back to times when they've tried to solve a tough challenge or achieve big aspirations. Then we ask them to answer that third question, "What makes it hard to close The Gap between concerns and aspirations?"

Their answers reveal why many of us are content to live with the current, sometimes downright dismal, reality. These are what makes progress hard:

- Entrenched viewpoints
- Inability to get people to agree on what the problem really is
- Everybody having a different opinion about what the solution should be
- The pressure to make a profit
- The pressure to serve in the way we've always served
- People in authority who don't want to change how they operate
- Complacency
- Apathy
- Competing values
- Interpersonal conflicts

Some acknowledge their own part of the mess, their own contributions to maintaining the status quo. They talk about their fears and frequent inability to intervene effectively to move things forward.

They acknowledge what stops them from seizing more moments to lead:

- I get too overwhelmed.
- I get stressed and can't think straight.
- I'm afraid to speak up.
- I avoid talking with people who don't think like me.
- I feel powerless.
- I can't stand disruption.
- Those who hired me can't stand disruption.
- Those who elected me want me to do what they want rather than explore what's best for the community as a whole.
- I can't stand to disappoint people.
- I can't stand conflict.
- I can't stand rejection.
- I get mired in the details and the daily grind.
- Do I care enough to risk doing something differently?
- I care about everything, so I do nothing.

Sound familiar?

When people talk about what makes it hard to bridge The Gap, they describe the characteristics of adaptive challenges:

- There is no clear solution. Instead you need to be ready to learn and understand the situation from multiple perspectives.

- Authority and expertise are not enough. You need all the right stakeholders engaged and ready to exercise leadership.

- The work is not efficient or straightforward. It's about curiosity, experimentation, and learning.

- Progress rarely happens quickly. It takes time, patience, and a strong sense of purpose.

When the challenge is adaptive, we have to engage with people who think differently than we do. We have to manage our own insecurities to do what is needed rather than what is comfortable. We have to acknowledge the barriers to progress but never let them get us down. We have to think strategically, stay curious, be open to learn, and be ready to experiment our way across The Gap.

Don't Treat Your Toughest Challenges Like Technical Problems

Too often we treat adaptive challenges as if they were technical problems.

Technical problems are easy to recognize because you know the steps to solve them or can depend on someone else to solve them. Technical problems live in people's heads. You solve them by gathering facts and using authority or expertise.

Adaptive challenges, on the other hand, are not clearly defined. People need to be curious and seek new ways to understand what is going on. Solutions demand developing new tools, methods, and ways of communicating. Progress on big, daunting, adaptive challenges takes time, willpower, and patience. You can see why there is always pressure to interpret challenges as technical problems.

When everyone leads, people throughout your organization are working to distinguish technical and adaptive work.

	TECHNICAL	ADAPTIVE
PROBLEM	clear	requires learning
SOLUTION	clear	requires learning
WHOSE WORK IS IT?	experts, authority	stakeholders
TYPE OF WORK	efficient	act experimentally
TIMELINE	ASAP	longer term
EXPECTATIONS	fix problem	make progress
ATTITUDE	confidence, skill	curiosity

Our biggest, most important challenges almost always feature a mix of both technical and adaptive. Eventually you'll want everyone asking questions like, "What aspects of this situation are technical and can be solved by bringing in the right expert or spending money in the right place?" And "What aspects are adaptive and demand further diagnosis and conversation with stakeholders?"

Distinguish Technical From Adaptive

If the problem is solely technical, bring expertise and skill:

- WiFi in the corporate headquarters is down. The solution is for the building manager to get their technicians working on the problem. Those technicians have training and expertise to solve the problem as fast as possible.

- A jet bridge malfunctions and passengers are unable to depart. The solution is to get the mechanic there as quickly as possible and give him the time to fix the problem.

- A young professional is facilitating her first team check-in. She wants to ensure everyone gets a chance to report on their work for the coming week. It's essential that the meeting last no more than 30 minutes. The solution to her problem is asking a more senior colleague with a reputation for running productive meetings for advice about designing the agenda.

The problems and solutions in these examples are straightforward and simple. You might not know how to fix the jet bridge or draft a good agenda, but someone does. Compare these examples to the concerns and aspirations explored in the last few chapters. Our biggest concerns point to challenges that are primarily adaptive. They are complex, multifaceted, and—for the most part—resist easy descriptions or solutions.

No doubt, technical work is necessary to keep things running smoothly and efficiently. But it's the adaptive challenges in your organization, company, or community that are crying out for more leadership. You'll make more progress when everyone is asking, "Is our challenge technical, adaptive, or some combination of both?"

MAKING IT REAL

> **Dear Ed and Julia,**
>
> I am a nurse and the coordinator of schedules in our hospital's emergency department. I need to get all the nurses on the same page about how we fill vacant shifts. I bring people together to try to talk about how to manage the schedule, but the discussionkeeps going off the rails. People spend the time talking about how exhausted they are and how they feel under-appreciated by doctors and hospital administrators. After the meeting I'm still scrambling to cover last-minute absences. Most of the time I end up covering them myself. Help me. I'm exhausted too! What does leadership look like here?
>
> **—Kai Can't Take It Anymore**

Dear Kai,

You've offered a great example of a complex challenge that has aspects that are technical and some that are adaptive. The primary technical piece seems to be how to fill the shifts. You can address that using your authority as the coordinator (the expert, the person in charge). Don't give that work to the other nurses. Decide how the schedule is going to work and hold people accountable for doing their part. Get some help from a boss or mentor if you don't have all the skills or information you need to set up a system that works. Sometimes technical work like this is enough. It satisfies people, calms things down, and eliminates the problem. But from what you've told us, there are deeper dilemmas here.

Some aspects of your challenge defy easy solutions. Beyond the nuts and bolts of schedules, what might be the deeper reasons your discussions are going off the rails? Does the uproar around how you fill vacant shifts symbolize something bigger about the culture? We wonder if your challenge is about keeping emergency room nurses engaged and motivated to do their best work when they feel exhausted, overwhelmed, or even underappreciated.

For now, the best leadership moves may be listening and tryingto determine what you can fix using your authority and whataspects of the challenge are adaptive and will require engagingother people. Listen—at the nurses' station and in the cafeteria—to how your colleagues are feeling. Instead of talking aboutschedules, consider using meeting time to ask the questionsfrom Chapter 5. Even if it is not in your job description, start learning as much as you can about what motivates anddemotivates nurses in your department. Keep going back to the chart from this chapter, and keep asking yourself: What about this situation is technical? And what is adaptive?

Part Two

Barriers to Progress

If you have ever tried to tackle an entrenched, daunting problem, you know how hard it is to find the way forward. There is no clear path. Barriers abound. The work of dealing with them is messy and hard. With adaptive challenges, even your best attempts to get things unstuck don't work or are woefully inadequate.

The barriers to progress aren't illusions. Failing to address them makes our biggest problems even worse. But most people would rather not deal with the things that make leadership difficult. They'd rather side-step a tough conversation or put off listening to someone with a different opinion. Too many people choose comfort over leadership.

But those who really want to solve the most daunting challenges do not turn away from The Gap. Instead they get to know the five big barriers to progress so they can mobilize others to find the way around them.

In the next five chapters we describe common barriers to progress on adaptive challenges. As you read, you'll discover—as we have—that progress on adaptive challenges requires:

1. Navigating loss
2. Reordering values
3. Resisting the allure of a quick fix
4. More than authority (leadership from the many, not the few)
5. Managing risk

Most of us are grasping for ways to solve the complex challenges facing our organizations and communities. When more people recognize the barriers, we will make more progress on what matters most.

7
Our Toughest Challenges Involve Loss

When Ron Heifetz talks about adaptive challenges, he uses evolution as a metaphor. Similar to the way species adapt (aka change) to fit their environment, so too must our organizations, companies, and communities adapt to survive and thrive. Adaptation isn't just a process of adding, but also of subtracting, of letting go. To get across The Gap to our new, better reality, we have to be willing to take some loss.

We spent time researching the 2008 global financial meltdown to help wrap our minds around these ideas of loss, massive change, and forced adaptation. We found that the organizations that thrived through the crisis were ones that both retrenched and invested. By *retrenching* we mean they acknowledged, understood, and accepted necessary losses. They made cuts and focused scarce resources where they were needed most. Unlike companies that failed or barely survived the crisis, the successful companies didn't just hunker down. They prioritized innovation. They took risks. Even in the midst of a crisis, they invested in new ways forward.

Those companies understood that progress on our most important challenges requires letting go of some things so we can lean into others.

The 2008 financial crisis, like the COVID-19 pandemic, created massive change, but the pressure to evolve has been building for years. The rate of change has accelerated sofast in recent decades that the need to adapt is nearly constant. We are always adjusting to our own losses and helping other people deal with theirs.

People Hate Change Because They Fear Loss

On the one hand, people crave change. We imagine what life would be like after winning the Mega Millions jackpot lottery. We root for our political party to win, believing in its message of change. We long for the big contract that will dramatically change our department at work, allowing us finally to expand the team and make more impact.

On the other hand, we are told people are afraid of change. It's the mantra you hear anytime you talk with someone who is getting resistance to their big, shiny idea.

What gives? Here's one way to think about it:

We love change that has only upside.

- A department receives 300 percent more budget authority to put in place those big plans the employees have been dreaming up.

- A college sports team changes leagues and now will play on national television every week, bringing more attention and glory to the team and fanbase.

- A local billionaire gives all her money to create new arts organizations, parks, and amenities for the community to enjoy without tax increases.

Everyone loves those types of change.

But we hate change that brings loss.

- A department must merge with another, creating efficiencies for the company but likely leading to 50 percent layoffs.

- A college sports team sees other teams leave the league for better competition and more television revenue. The league will be weakened, and the team will get less attention and less television revenue.

- A community has decided to raise taxes by $500 million to invest in parks and recreation amenities. Citizens like the positives for the community but have second thoughts when they see changes to tax bills.

When facing an adaptive challenge, most people take a quick glance—see the loss, conflict, and discomfort—and look the other way. The inability to deal with the loss that comes with change is a major barrier to progress on our toughest challenges.

Why Is It Hard to Accept That Change Requires Loss?

We want to believe that we can create change but avoid the loss.
We lie to ourselves and one another about the losses that come
with progress on tough challenges:

- **Authorities tell us we can have our cake and eat it too.**
  We've grown accustomed to politicians telling us we can have
  all upside and no downside. We want to believe it's possible.

- **People in authority are not trained to help others
  navigate loss.** They lack skills like speaking with empathy,
  deep listening, and knowing how to pace the change.

- **We are conditioned to avoid the negative.** We focus on
  the rosy change, not the unfortunate loss. We don't let our
  minds go there.

- **We hate disappointing people.** We don't want to create
  conflict or stoke anger. Helping others face loss takes courage
  we don't have.

- **Sometimes the loss is our own.** For example, for your
  organization to refocus on its mission, you might have to let go
  of a program or a piece of your role that defines you. When the
  challenges are adaptive, no one gets a free pass.

Research shows people feel more pain in losing something they
already have than they do pleasure from gaining something of
the same or greater value. Likewise, individuals will often even

ignore the evidence of their own senses if it allows them to go along with the group. When facing a tough challenge, we exert pressure on ourselves and one another to avoid loss and maintain the status quo.

What Happens When We Accept Loss as Part of Change?

Accepting that solving our most important challenges involves loss opens the door for lasting change. When we link change with loss, we can:

- **Seek to understand losses for ourselves and other people.**

- **Look for ways to mitigate and help people deal with loss.** For more about helping others navigate the loss that comes with change, see the "Speak to Loss" chapter in Ed's book *Your Leadership Edge*.

- **Pace the work.** Helping people deal with loss takes time. Too many initiatives fail because the change agents didn't appreciate the loss involved.

The potential for loss keeps us stuck. It creates resistance to change. On the other hand, understanding the link between change and loss energizes people. It makes us more patient when things take time. Dealing with loss may slow us down at first. But ultimately it helps make change stick.

Everyone Needs to Understand the Relationship Between Loss and Change

Change happens faster when a critical mass of people connect accepting loss with making progress on their most important challenges. Once people understand that connection, they will be more likely to exercise leadership, in their own way, to help name, understand, and mitigate the loss that comes with change. When everyone leads, we help each other navigate loss.

MAKING IT REAL

Dear Ed and Julia,

I'm part of a coalition of civic groups (Chamber of Commerce, Visitor's Bureau, Community Foundation, etc.) that is pushing for a massive redevelopment of property downtown. The plans we've created call for exciting amenities that will make our community more attractive for young professionals, businesses, and families. But the resistance from those who want to keep things the same is exhausting! They don't have ideas of their own. They're just against everything we propose! We've been at this for years and I'm beginning to fear no resolution is in sight. Why is this so hard?

—Soren Seeking Solutions

Dear Soren,

People don't resist things they think are wonderful. Your changes must represent loss to these opponents. You won't win them over by preaching why your plan is right. Leadership here is understanding their perceived or real loss and mitigating that loss as much as possible.

You've been at this for years and will likely struggle for years more unless you engage opponents differently. What might they lose? Maybe your plan takes down historic buildings they care about. Maybe your plan diverts energy and tax resources from other parts of the city they fear will be neglected.

Unless your group simply has unilateral power (unlikely given you've been at this awhile), leadership is engaging these other factions, not complaining about them. Maybe some of their fears are valid and you need to adjust your plan.

It won't be easy. But that's what leadership on adaptive challenges looks like.

8
Values Clash When You Seek to Close The Gap

Progress stalls on an adaptive challenge when your team fails to address a values conflict. There is no shame in competing values. It's human to want two or more things at once. The problem comes when conflicting values go unaddressed, concerns grow deeper, and big aspirations remain just that.

Consider these situations:

- A married couple says they value higher education for their children, but their savings account tells a different story. There's nothing there. The battle here is between the espoused value for "higher education" and the real value for "vacations and late model vehicles."

- A political candidate claims he values voters across the state but spends most of his campaign time and money in the rural areas. Once elected, his agenda focuses on rural interests more than urban and suburban interests. The battle here is between the espoused value for "every voter" and the real value for "the voters that put me in office."

- A company claims it values collaboration, but managers claim credit for their team's good ideas and salespeople keep the hottest leads to themselves. Furthermore, the executive team awards big bonuses to stand-out performers, leaving team members grumbling when their contributions go unrecognized. The battle for the executive team is between the espoused value of "teamwork" and the real value of "pleasing the people we don't want snatched away."

When the challenge is adaptive a group has to renegotiate the relationship between two values. But people don't like to talk frankly about which values get attention and which get lip service. One value we happily proclaim to the world. We put it on our brochures and the wall of our boardroom. The other feels less noble. It might be about our organization's survival, team members' insecurities, or a desire to keep our company culture intact. One value is talked about but not fully acted upon. The second exerts a silent opposition to the first. To oversimplify, when a group is facing a tough challenge one value is "winning"; another value is "losing." The unseen battle slows everything down.

When Progress Stalls, Examine Values

An unexamined value clash could be draining energy from your change initiative.

Here's another example: An executive team says diversity and inclusion are important. They tell themselves they value new perspectives and intend to diversify their team someday. But they think they just don't have time to make it happen now. They need to fill a critical open position and it turns out that Billy and Sarah, whom they've known for years and who have a background just like theirs, are perfect candidates. The team decides there's no need for a search.

In this situation values clashed and "fill the position now" won. If this company's toughest challenge is developing a more diverse, inclusive workforce, the executive team has perfected the art of making excuses.

For these two values to get equal attention, people throughout the company will have to merge the drive for diversity with the business imperative to fill open positions. That may look like tolerating the pain of an open job search longer. It may require more time to be spent developing new networks and fewer job postings in the usual places. Addressing the clash of values means focusing as much energy on the *importance* of a diverse pool of candidates as on the *urgency* of filling the position.

Ways We Hide or Minimize Value Conflicts

People hide or minimize values conflicts in two common ways.

We claim we value something but don't allocate time or money to it. What we spend time and money on tells others what we value. We want to be seen as valuing all the noble things, so we say we favor one thing but don't spend enough time or money to achieve it.

- A city says it values parks but has decreased funding for parks for several years running. Council members could address this barrier to progress by openly discussing the tendency to value "no new taxes" over "parks in every neighborhood."

- A company says it values its overseas offices, yet senior executives never make time to visit them. International employees might get more engaged if executives openly discuss the value conflict. Most people would rather see authority wrestle with competing priorities than proceed in silent hypocrisy.

- A nonprofit board talks about how important it is to retain front-line workers, but the percentage of the budget allocated to their benefits shrinks every year. The board's behavior demonstrates exactly how much it really values those workers.

Too often we focus on where we agree and ignore the value conflicts. You know you have a tough adaptive challenge on your hands if there is total public agreement about a big goal or aspiration, yet progress is still elusive. People avoid dealing with competing values by telling one another "we're all on the same page." They go to sleep each night confident the tough work is behind them and wake up to another day in which nothing substantial gets done.

- A country claims to value pre-kindergarten education and childcare. People in local, regional, and national government talk about supporting early learning for all. Not one elected official is "opposed" to more funding. But there are always 57 things that demand higher priority.

- A governor commits himself to improving K–12 education in his state. He convenes task forces and conferences where speakers laud the nobility of the cause. But they avoid talking about the people who stand to lose with new approaches to education. Speakers paint a rosy future and don't address the clash of values between "comfort, predictability, and secure jobs for administrators and teachers" and the aspiration for "the best education system in the country."

- Managers at a regional social service organization are on board with a new structure designed to make the organization more competitive and win more contracts. But so far no one has asked how the changes are affecting low-income clients. They ignore the value clash between "win more contracts" and "listen to our people."

It's Not Selling Out

Progress on a tough challenge doesn't require you to be a sellout. We don't need to disregard one thing we value and go all in with something else. We just need to be willing—for a while—to value one thing a little less so we can value the other thing a little more. We need to spend less time and fewer resources in one place so we can devote more energy to the thing that matters most.

Value Clashes Require Leadership from the Many, Not the Few

Painting your company values on the wall of the boardroom doesn't make them your values.

Words on the wall are just words. Real values are those that people at all levels of your organization embrace and act upon. Real values aren't settled upon in one meeting. The question "What does your group value?" gets answered in hundreds of choices made by people every day.

If you want your organization to successfully meet its most important challenges, you'll need lots of people who can:

- Name the value driving a decision.

- Acknowledge competing values.

- Lean into conversations about how to navigate conflicting values.

You'll close The Gap faster when everyone wonders,"Does what we're doing match all the talk about what we care about most?"

When everyone leads, people at all levels in your organization, community, or family feel empowered to name those hidden priorities. They look for moments to ask questions about whether the group is walking its talk. Everyone feels compelled to do what they can to develop a common understanding of what matters most. When everyone leads, we stop depending on the person in authority to see everything, catch every misalignment, and say all the hard things.

MAKING IT REAL

> **Dear Ed and Julia,**
>
> I'm the city manager of a large municipality with an aging infrastructure. For years we've known our water pipes throughout town need critical repairs and replacements. One hundred percent of the pipes are at risk of critical failure. But solving this situation requires an investment of at least $200 to $300 million. The city council has been unwilling to entertain using their political capital for such an investment. In the meantime, however, we've built a new baseball stadium, have expanded parks, and are planning a new performing arts center. The price tag of those items significantly exceeds the water project. What does leadership look like for this situation?
>
> **—Willie from Waterville**

Willie,

Our guess is your city council will surely say it values the water infrastructure. But proof is in the pudding, right? Their willingness to fund the stadium and other projects suggests a classic battle of competing values. They appear to value things that can be seen and that are shiny and new compared to mundane things that can't be seen. Water pipes are mundane. Maybe council members worry their bosses (the voters) won't be as impressed with the hidden water pipes as they are with new amenities.

Leadership here looks like helping lots of people (the elected officials, city staff, political heavyweights in the community, etc.) see and talk about the value choice clearly. A key question we encourage you to ask often is this: We say we value solving the water problem, but what actions or investments would back up that talk?

9
Quick Fixes Don't Work

It's easy to trick ourselves into believing we can solve our biggest challenge but avoid the discomfort that comes with adaptive work.

Maybe you are facing a challenge and have identified a promising quick fix. Yes, definitely, explore that idea! But be warned: It could be a diversion. Progress always takes more time than we want to admit.

Think about it this way: It took months, years, or even decades to create the problem (i.e., declining sales, increasing homeless population, a family feud, etc.) or the opportunity in front of you (diversifying the community's economy, merging two companies into a stronger whole, making your organization more inclusive). A multitude of factors created your current situation, so it will take many shifts, big and small, to create lasting change.

The Seductive Quick Fix

Even the most well-meaning people can get seduced and led astray by our craving for a speedy solution to a big, daunting, adaptive challenge. For example,

- Topline revenue at a tech company has leveled off and softening sales of its flagship product are to blame. Progress will require new levels of investment in innovation throughout the company. However, when new resources become available, rather than using them to drive new product development, senior authorities triple the marketing budget for the flagship product. Meanwhile, the adaptive work of igniting a culture of innovation moves to the back burner. Several quarters later, no significant improvements have been made in either revenue or innovation. The Gap is bigger than ever before.

- A school's students are dramatically underperforming when it comes to the number of third graders reading at grade-level. Progress will require an assortment of interventions in the school, the neighborhood, faith communities, and families. School board members get seduced by a new reading curriculum. They dedicate significant chunks of their tight budget to teacher training, new books, and resources for the program. The lure of the quick fix distracts everyone from the need for more comprehensive interventions.

- A church is steadily losing members. Young people are rarely in the pews. Progress will require multiple efforts, including listening to young people and discerning why the message, traditions, and practices of the church aren't connecting. But there's no time for that discernment because all available resources are being poured into a new service with a praise band and video boards. Meanwhile, two young couples leave the congregation and the problem gets worse as the group delays deeper diagnosis.

In most cases, a seductive quick fix is one in which you are putting all of your eggs in one basket. If we fall for the allure of the quick fix, knowingly or not, we broadcast a message to our whole system that it is okay to stop being curious, stop innovating, and slow down learning. We may even inadvertently send the message that there is no adaptive challenge, no complexity to deal with, no dangerous pressures to navigate. If we decide we've got this handled, we risk making The Gap between concerns and aspirations larger instead of smaller. A quick fix diverts attention from our most important challenge and makes it more difficult than ever for people to find unique ways to contribute to creating meaningful change.

Avoid the Trap by Understanding the Allure

We may be devoted to the mission and success of our organization or company and still fall into the trap of the quick fix. We may jump at what looks like a painless solution and avoid the inevitable adaptive work.

There are good reasons to love the quick fix:

1. **It lets us off the hook.** Applying a quick fix diverts our gaze from The Gap and allows us to move onto something else. The quick fix allows us to avoid messy, uncomfortable work like dealing with other factions and upsetting people we care about. A quick fix lets us off the hook by letting us think we're done.

2. **We get to do what we are good at.** When we choose a quick fix, it's usually an approach we are comfortable with. When instead we resist the allure, we hold ourselves in a state of disequilibrium. Curiosity is the only way forward. How many of us are willing to admit publicly that we don't know how to solve a daunting challenge? We'd rather apply a solution from our back pocket than admit we have a lot to learn.

3. **It satisfies the people we need to please.** Avoiding the allure of the quick fix is especially hard for people who need votes (or approval from a board of directors) to keep their job. People expect those in authority to keep everything under control. No boss or elected official wants to make a speech saying that the solution to
a tough challenge will require hard work from everyone, that everyone will have to give up something, and that progress will be incremental.

No matter who you are and how much experience you have, it will be tempting to look at what concerns you the most, grab the quick fix, and convince yourself you've closed The Gap. Once in a great while—usually in cases in which your challenge is more technical than adaptive—the quick fix works. If the challenge is adaptive, don't count on it.

Beyond the Quick Fix: Leadership from the Many, Not the Few

Once everyone in your system understands the allure of the quick fix, three things start to happen:

1. **You run more experiments.** When we reject the quick fix, we stop putting all our eggs in one basket. Instead of investing all extra resources into a marketing campaign, for instance, if our challenge is stagnant product development, we would run multiple experiments to encourage innovation in every department. Yes, product designers would need to think differently, but everyone else would need to imagine new ways of working together too. Employees will view each intervention as an experiment rather than a "fix" and will invest only limited resources until they know which experiments hold the most promise of success.

2. **You set better timetables.** When we accept that a quick fix won't lead to lasting change, we get more realistic about our expectations. We set benchmarks that acknowledge the adaptive nature of the work and find moments to celebrate progress along the way.

3. You stop overpromising and start overdelivering. When people attempt quick fixes they are prone to overpromise: the boss promises that the merger will be painless, the mayor promises that if everyone wears masks the pandemic will be over soon, the president promises a quick end to a recession. Expectations get absurdly high. When we understand the allure of the quick fix, we are more likely to underpromise and overdeliver, a better recipe for healthy relationships and successful change initiatives.

As more people appreciate the complexities of adaptive work, they stop believing that one person should know the answer and start wondering how they can contribute. Thinking beyond the quick fix creates room for more people to get involved, to seize their moment, and to lead.

MAKING IT REAL

Dear Ed and Julia,

I am the owner of a business in a rural town far from a major urban area. Two of our six employees are quitting. There aren't many qualified local people for these positions. Lots of businesses face this problem. It's hard to get people to move to this part of the state and hard to keep them. Recruitment and retention of employees are my biggest challenges. I'm about to sign a contract with an out-of-state staffing firm, hoping that will finally solve this for me. Any other thoughts about what leadership looks like in this situation?

—Lev Who Is Tired of People Leaving

Dear Lev,

The contract with the staffing firm might make sense. But it sounds a lot like a quick fix. That firm will help you fill those roles, but it sounds like the revolving door is a constant problem. We can't imagine that the staffing firm can do much to help with retention or the lack of locally qualified workers.

Leadership here probably looks like exploring more lasting solutions. Engage people to work on the challenge long-term. Who else cares about bringing skilled workers to your region or retraining those who are already there? What experiments could you run that could set your company and community up for long-lasting success?

Consider exploring a partnership between local businesses and a nearby community college to provide people already living in the community a chance to learn the skills needed in area businesses.

The contract with the staffing firm might be needed, but it won't solve anything in the long run. Lean into leadership on this one. Years from now, your company and community will be thankful you did.

10
Authority Is Never Enough to Close The Gap

Let's lean into this disquieting notion that even if you are the CEO (or the governor, prime minister, or president), when the challenge is adaptive, your authority alone will never be enough to bridge The Gap. Progress on adaptive challenges requires those in authority to do their part, but their part alone is insufficient for progress.

Imagine a vice president for human resources who wants to stop employees from turning in leave "requests" after they have already taken the time off. She can take steps to solve that problem. She can force a change of behavior by simply issuing a policy saying requests will be denied when they are submitted after the leave has been taken. She can dock employee pay as a result of violating the policy. Things will change quickly when she deploys her authority because the challenge is technical and she is the one in charge.

If the problem is technical, we solve it by using our own authority or leveraging someone else's. If the challenge is adaptive, however, that authority isn't enough. People in authority must take a different approach to instigating change.

Now imagine that same vice president is tasked by the CEO with fostering more creativity throughout the company. In this scenario no similar roadmap, no quick use of authority can force that type of change. She can't issue a directive or institute a creativity policy and expect to see results. To some extent the VP's authority and access to budget and other resources is useful. She can convene a series of conversations with a range of stakeholders, asking openended questions about barriers to creativity in the company. She can bring in speakers and conduct workshops on creativity. She can suggest that "evidence of creative solutions to problems" be added to the end-of-year performance bonus rubric. She can buy copies of *Creative Confidence* by brothers Tom and David Kelley and host a series of book club discussions with employees. All these actions could be useful, but none can guarantee progress toward a more creative company.

Instead, progress requires lots of employees up and down the org chart each deciding to do a thing or two differently in the spirit of fostering more creativity. Closing The Gap could happen in a million combinations of ways: It could look like more managers creating meeting agendas that revolve around open-ended questions rather than department updates, or more individual contributors deciding to try a new approach to a project, even if it means it will take a bit longer to finish. Her authority is useful, but not sufficient.

Our systems place enormous (often unspoken) expectations on people in authority to treat problems as technical. But if the VP makes that mistake here, the company misses countless opportunities for other people to offer ways forward.

When groups wait for those at the top to fix problems that are adaptive, they waste precious time and resources.

Leadership and Authority Are Not the Same Thing

Leadership is an activity. A thing we do. Leadership is mobilizing others to make progress on complex and entrenched challenges. It is not a role.

Authority is a position. People hold it. And always, if we are talking about the really hairy adaptive challenges, no one person is powerful enough to exercise all the leadership all by themselves.

We are not saying get rid of all the presidents, pastors, board chairs, and CEOs. Far from it! The world needs people in positions of authority. Communities elect and appoint them for a reason. Organizations recruit and hire them to provide structure and to help people feel content and secure enough to show up every day and do good work. Authorities need to cast vision and set direction, but that's not enough for progress on adaptive challenges.

Perhaps you are the person in authority. You've been hired (or elected or appointed) to a lofty position. Those who chose you for the job expect you to direct the way forward. Others look to you for the sense of order they need to feel secure about their place in the world. They want you to make it easy for them to succeed and protect them from outside threats. If the right people stay happy, you keep your job.

Therefore the temptation for the person in charge is to treat every challenge as something to be fixed fast or pushed aside. With an adaptive challenge, this approach may calm things down in the short term, but it won't really solve the problem. Progress on our most important challenges almost always involves doing something disruptive to move people off the status quo.

Big Change Happens When Everyone Leads

Big change is only possible when we release our dependence on authority. Big change comes when each of us steps up to see and seize our moments to lead.

When everyone embraces the idea that authority is not enough to make progress on our most important challenges:

- **We are more likely to consider our own part of the mess or piece of the puzzle.** If you are in authority, you begin to understand that your role is less about solving the problem yourself and more about creating the conditions for others to exercise leadership. If you are not in authority, you realize that you can be an active participant in change.

- **Attention will focus on the whole system, rather than just those in authority.** You and your colleagues will see that closing The Gap (i.e., reversing downward sales numbers, finally creating one culture out of two organizations that merged years ago, increasing graduation rates, etc.) is a challenge each can own and influence from a unique perspective.

- **Interventions from authority look different.** Rather than telling others how he sees the problem and what his solution is, an executive would engage his team with questions: What concerns you about this situation? What contributes to the problem? Who needs to do what to make progress on this? Who else?

Why Is It Hard to Accept That Authority Is Insufficient?

There are three main reasons we resist this idea that authority is insufficient to bridge The Gap:

1. We want someone to come to our rescue.

2. We like to blame people in authority for our problems.

3. If we are the one in the top job, we don't want to disappoint people.

We want to believe if we just elect, appoint, or hire the right person everything will be solved. We want to believe that if someone in authority fails to solve a tough problem we can simply throw that person out and find someone better to take their place. And because people want to be rescued, people in positions of authority buy into the idea that solving the adaptive challenges is their responsibility. They trick themselves into believing they can make change by themselves. They don't want to disappoint the people who hired or elected them. They certainly don't want to lose their jobs.

Too many have been conditioned to think that because the person in authority is getting paid the most, they should come up with the answers. That might suffice for technical problems, but with our most important adaptive challenges, it just won't work. For those not in authority, this adds pressure on you. When you realize that efforts by your boss (or your mayor or rabbi or committee chair) are insufficient, it puts a spotlight on you. Everyone (not just the person in authority) will need to stretch beyond their comfort zone to seize moments to exercise leadership.

MAKING IT REAL

Dear Ed and Julia,

I am a physician with 30 years of experience in a teaching hospital. Conflict between residents in training and floor nurses is threatening the hospital's strong reputation in the community. There are nurses who don't trust residents to know what they are doing and for that reason, I suppose, they fail to convey important information to these young physicians. The problem keeps getting worse. Now we are struggling to recruit residents and nurses. I plan to talk with the nursing administration and see if they can have nurses held accountable to tell me what is really happening. How do I use my authority to fix this?

—Denis the Doctor

Dear Denis,

Hang in there. You are doing a lot of things right and a little shift of perspective will go a long way. Is this really a problem you could fix if you had power over the nurses? What if this is an adaptive challenge requiring leadership from a lot more people?

All the expertise or power in the world is not enough to fix this one. Get in The Gap with those nurses and try to understand things from their point of view. Maybe start talking about leadership as an activity. Ask open-ended questions and really listen to the answers. Encourage nurses and residents to risk speaking directly to one another. See what happens as you commit to a culture where everyone leads.

11
Leadership Is Risky

Exercising leadership on your toughest challenge is like having a one-way ticket on an ocean liner bound for a country where you've never been. Risks and uncertainty abound.

Julia's grandmother, Gerolima, and her 10-year-old son boarded the SS Rex in Genoa in 1937 and set off for Cleveland, Ohio, to reunite with her husband for the first time since the boy was born. She didn't know much about the life she was going to or what the risks of the crossing would be. The loss, on the other hand, of people and places she'd always known, was palpable. Her husband was a young man when he left to find work in America a decade before. His letters tried to describe the wood-frame house on a crowded street not far from downtown. But Gerolima couldn't comprehend how different a Great Lakes steel city would be from the tiny Adriatic island that had been their families' home for centuries. She couldn't know what aspects of her new life would thrill or distress her, whether neighbors would welcome or reject her, or whether their son would thrive. She couldn't know how they would all make a life together after

10 painful years apart. Yet, in spite of the risks, Gerolima boarded that ocean liner and spent a week on the open sea.

When exercising leadership, we can't be sure of the outcome. Once you start to intervene—to exercise leadership—you can't be sure exactly where the risk will come from or when it will show up. That's why you need to get good at seeing and managing the risks associated with exercising leadership on your challenge. The journey ends if you don't. You never reach dry land and the concerns that propelled you in the first place remain or—more likely—get worse.

Consider these examples:

- A small business acquired a one-year contract as a supplier to a large manufacturer. If all goes well in year one, the business can expect a multiyear contract to follow. But many in the small business are tense. Management thinks it's a recipe for disaster if they attempt the new contract without discontinuing some work elsewhere. Everyone is already stretched so thin. The risk is trying to do too much and therefore not doing anything well enough. But then again, discontinuing some work feels risky too.

- An advocacy organization struggles to make inroads because no one on their board or staff has relationships or connections with policy makers who don't automatically align with their views. The organization has allowed a culture of "different perspective = political enemy" to flourish unchecked, in part because there are real risks associated with building relationships across factions: What if the media gets wind of a staff member engaged in authentic conversation or, worse, being influenced, just a little bit, by someone from "the other side"?

- City council members in a rural community seek to make the area more welcoming for newcomers, including those from the big city. But those elected officials risk backlash (and expulsion from their seats) from voters whose families have been in the community forever and who believe they shouldn't have to change anything to make things comfortable for new residents. From the perspectives of some locals, those who move into the town can either "like it or leave it."

Progress on our most important challenges always requires a letting go, a loss, so we can move forward. In whatever system you work or volunteer, you and others have cocreated ways of engaging and functioning that work well enough to get the daily tasks done and, at least for now, keep the lights on and the doors open. People have their ways of doing things and they have become accustomed to them.

But a tree's leaves must die and fall before new growth emerges in the spring. A controlled burn every few years allows the prairie ecosystem to thrive.

Leadership is an activity that involves mobilizing people to let go of habits and norms that no longer serve them. That kind of letting go is uncomfortable. Most people would rather put off hard and uncomfortable things.

So, by nature, leadership is risky. Trying to change things—even if the end goal is to make things better for everyone—takes will and courage.

No Risk = No Leadership

Politicians demonstrate risk aversion better than anyone. And how their followers react to their behavior shows why it is so hard to do things that risk upsetting your own people. A politician speaks to a massive crowd of supporters, raising her voice when angrily deriding her opponent and the other political party. Her speech stirs the hearts and minds of her faithful supporters, effectively landing her message points. The speech ends with a crescendo of passion and the crowd erupts in applause. The people love it and reward the politician at the ballot box. Although the scene might be great politics, it's not leadership. Nothing about that scene was risky.

Risky would be telling the crowd they own part of the problem too and need to fix their part of the mess.

Whatever your context, the odds are high that your team is contributing something to the existence of the group's biggest challenge. Perhaps those closest to you are failing to make necessary changes or refusing to relinquish norms that get in the way of progress. Pointing that out is risky. Continuing to point it out is riskier. Trying to get your own people to address their piece of the challenge carries with it some danger that must be taken into account.

Why don't more of us suck it up and take the necessary risks associated with exercising leadership? There are three common reasons:

1. **Our purpose isn't clear enough.** Sometimes we haven't done enough work to define our leadership challenge. Therefore the idea of risking anything to bridge The Gap between the current reality and our aspirations seems foolhardy. So we don't act.

2. **We overinflate the risks.** Oftentimes we convince ourselves that necessary risks threaten our livelihood, reputation, membership in a community, even our identity. But the real risks are usually less dire. They are more related to pride and ego. We fail to act for fear of undermining our sense of confidence and competence, or our sense of security about our value and place in the group.

3. **We've taken risks before, and it didn't go well.** If this is the case for you, take heart. The mindset you are developing as you read this book, the inspiration to contribute to groups where everyone leads, and the new skills you can develop to support your leadership will serve you well for the future.

How Much Risk Is Too Much?

We are not encouraging you to risk everything. Granted, a politician who chooses to shift away from a conquering hero model of leadership could set herself up for a challenging reelection campaign. But most of us do not have to put our livelihood or important relationships at risk when we choose to take a different approach to leadership on a tough challenge.

You don't want to find yourself on the outside, unable to have an impact on anything at all. So don't let yourself come to represent something people would rather not face, and don't risk so much that you become the symbol for the change people are resisting. If you do, people may pointtheir frustration toward you.

For example, imagine you are the sibling that keeps bringing up the need to reconcile with a sister who has become distant. If other family members are perfectly fine not seeing that sister, not only will they resist reconciliation, but they may start to resist you because you represent an issue they don't want to deal with.

But, with some attention, you can navigate and mitigatethe risks that come with leadership. Here's a set of quick tips for limiting your risk:

- Pace your efforts. Disappoint your own people at a rate they can handle.

- Be as consistent and dependable as you can. Don't completely upend key people's expectations of you.

- Try your leadership experiments one at a time and learn from each.

- Get feedback from trusted mentors and friends on your possible interventions before you try them.

- Admit your part of the mess first (and often). Only after you do so should you push people to consider their part of the mess.

- Regularly suggest incremental and evolutionary change. Save the big, wholesale change for key moments when the system is ripe.

- Don't create unrealistically short or exhaustingly long timelines for progress on entrenched challenges. Instead look for a few quick wins as you prepare peopleto engage with the challenge for a long time.

- Affirm people for wanting to jump to action even as you encourage them to spend more time in diagnosis.

- Don't tell people they are wrong. Instead, suggest that they might need to consider multiple perspectives and interpretations.

Risk will look different depending on where you sit in an organization. For a new employee, early in his career, it might feel risky to even ask a question in an all-company meeting. For a seasoned senior executive, it might feel risky to change things up because, after all, the current way of working propelled their success. If you are part of middle management, the risk might be making decisions you aren't sure you are authorized to make.

Getting in the game of solving our toughest problems becomes less risky when everyone leads.

Things that feel risky (speaking up at a meeting, proposing a new way forward, challenging the predominant interpretation for why things are the way they are, etc.) become less riskythe more they become the norm. That's the power when everyone leads. The culture of an organization, company, or community shifts and becomes more tolerant of the actions necessary for change and progress.

MAKING IT REAL

> **Dear Ed and Julia,**
>
> **Thanks for the list of dos and don'ts. I want to be brave but smart. What else can I do to make sure I don't take stupid risks?**
>
> **—Nadir Not Ready to Risk It All**

Dear Nadir,

If you look at the people who are most effective at tackling tough problems, you'll notice they have leadership skills that allow them to minimize, if not eliminate, risk. They learned those skills somewhere and they practice them every day. You can do the same. Surround yourself with people who understand the nature of adaptive challenges, watch how they intervene, and use them as models for how to exercise leadership that is less risky. The more you practice, the less risky leadership becomes.

Part Three

Start With You

So here you are. Your challenge is a messy one. It's got all the characteristics of an adaptive challenge. You've dealt with the technical stuff. Now what do you do?

If you are like most people, you fall into the trap of the quick fix: You throw some expertise at it and hope it sticks. Or you run it up the flagpole and pray somebody above you has the miracle cure.

If you are that person at the top of the flagpole, maybe you feel that pressure. You want to work miracles. Maybe you stay up all night drafting a plan. You dot every "i" and cross every "t." You make a timeline and assign names to tasks. You rush to the office the next morning and start delegating. Or you gather the volunteers that evening and start assigning.

Wait! Hold up!

This is an adaptive challenge, remember? Technical fixes won't work. At least not for long. Even the CEO or board chair can't delegate their way out of this one. No one bridges The Gap in one heroic leap.

But somebody has to start. Somebody has to try to exercise leadership. It may as well be you. You see the challenge for what it is: complex and adaptive. If you expect others to exercise leadership, you have to be willing to do it yourself. You have to get your hands dirty.

If you want to see more leadership happening in your company, organization, neighborhood, community, or country, you have to do your part. You'll eliminate barriers and make more progress on your toughest challenges when you do these five things:

1. **Start authorizing yourself to lead.** Empower yourself to exercise leadership. You are the only one who sees what you see and knows what you know. Use it. Don't wait for someone else to see it. Seize the moment to lead.

2. **Start with the challenge.** Forget the old leadership models. Put the adaptive challenge at the center of your work.

3. **Start where you have influence.** Lead where you are and where you can make a difference. Don't worry if it doesn't seem like much or if you aren't sure if it will make a difference.

4. **Start with your part of the mess.** Focus on your contribution to the situation—the good, the bad, and the in-between.

5. **Start engaging others.** Leadership is group work. Don't fly solo.

12
Start Authorizing Yourself to Lead

Whether you are a CEO, middle manager, mayor, governor, front-line employee, independent contributor, or community member, authorizing yourself to exercise leadership means deciding to do something above and beyond what's expected.

This chapter explores what that self-authorization looks like, how to do it, what makes it hard, and why it's necessary.

Our organizations, communities, and companies are held together by formal and informal hierarchies. Some of these are visible. We can see the org chart in the company. We can visit the city's website and see who serves on thecity council. Some are invisible. The middle manager who has been around for 20 years and has developed deep relationships up, down, and across the company likely holds as much as or more power than the new member of the executive team.

Here's a way of thinking about it. Imagine a circle with you in the middle. What's expected of you is in that circle. These might be formal expectations, like from a job description, or informal expectations, based on norms for people in your position. In the circle are the things you've been authorized to do.

Exercising leadership takes you outside the circle, outside of what's expected or what's been authorized. Here's what that looks like in real life:

- A student is expected to go to class, do homework, and follow the rules. Those things are inside the circle. When a student challenges the dress code, believing it treats some students and their cultural norms unfairly, she is outside the circle. She had to authorize herself to get there. No one was going to authorize her to intervene like that.

- An elected member of parliament is expected to toe the party line, give speeches using the party's talking points, vote with party members, and raise money for the party. Those things are inside the circle. When that member of parliament works with the opposition on a compromise bill, believing it's necessary for progress, they are outside the circle. They had to authorize themselves to get there. Those who authorized them (the loyal party voters who put them in office) aren't going to want them to intervene like that.

- After just a few months on the board of a mid-sized nonprofit, a new board member understands the board is expected to fundraise and do little else. Board members don't get involved with strategy or programs. At a board meeting, all heads turn when he asks, "What data shows this initiative is helping achieve our mission?" After a stunned silence other board members admit they have doubts about the program's impact. Asking provocative questions wasn't part of his stated responsibilities. No one was going to encourage him. He had to authorize himself.

You Have to Authorize Yourself

Leadership is a self-authorizing activity. No one else can authorize you to lead. Other people can tell you they want you to lead. They can put you in what they call a "leadership position" (what we call an *authority position*). But only you can make the intentional decision to try to exercise leadership.

The idea that leadership must be self-authorized is easier to grasp when you separate leadership from position and understand that leadership is an activity. Like any action, behavior, or activity, the person doing it needs to decide to do it. For instance,

- A new employee realizes leadership for her looks like intervening to help focus discussion. She decides it's up to her to ask the tough question in the staff meeting to get everyone focused on the elephant in the room.

- A longtime manager of a department realizes leadership for him looks like not answering every question from his staff. Instead, he holds back answers and asks them for ideas, creating space for his employees to discover solutions, many of which turn out better than his own. (We call this "giving the work back" and you can read more about it in *Your Leadership Edge*.)

- A community member, frustrated by unhealthy levels of polarization in the city, realizes leadership for them looks like modeling the kind of communication they want to see more of. They decide to invite community members with opposing views to conversations in which they get to know one another and search for common ground.

- The CEO of a regional Habitat for Humanity realizes that decision makers and big funders in her mid-sized city have little understanding of the impact of the 1940s-era government policies (known as *redlining*) on today's Black families; these policies kept their parents, grandparents, and great-grandparents from getting home loans. She starts inviting influencers to casual but provocative one-on-one tours of city neighborhoods.

Rarely do we lead by accident. It's almost always a conscious choice. It starts with deciding that not only *can* you lead, but to make progress, you *must* lead. You have to do your part.

Here are four reasons we fail to authorize ourselves to lead:

- **We worry we'll do something wrong and suffer consequences.** You might ask a provocative question but then get chastised for putting others on the spot. It can feel safer to sit on the sidelines and leave the tough work of leading to others.

- **The dominant view of leadership as a position keeps us stuck.** Everyone else is looking to authority to solve the problems and lead the way. We realize, consciously or subconsciously, that authorizing ourselves to lead, especially if we don't have authority, runs against the norm. Whether we admit it or not, most of us like to do what's expected.

- **We already have too much on our minds!** Being someone who exercises leadership means your mind is focused beyond what's expected of you. You have to be more alert and consider more perspectives. In the end your heightened curiosity will make progress on your challenge easier, faster, and more successful. But in the moment it may be simpler to keep your head down, and focus on what's already on your plate.

- **We miss the moments to lead.** If you can't see the moment to lead, it will be really hard to authorize yourself to do so.

What Happens When You Authorize Yourself to Lead

When you authorize yourself to lead, the benefits are personal and immediate:

- **You feel more engaged in your work, more satisfied and empowered.** Our research shows that employees who authorize themselves to lead, regardless of their job titles, are more committed to their organizations, more hopeful about their organizations' futures, and more satisfied with their jobs.

- **You no longer wait for permission to make things better.** You initiate change rather than wait to be told to do so by someone higher up. You ask difficult but important questions of peers and higher-ups.

- **You empower yourself to make a difference everywhere you go.** The idea that leadership is an activity has no boundaries. What you practice at work or as a community volunteer makes you a better friend, parent, niece, or neighbor.

- **You become part of the solution.** There is no doubt that your organization or community is dealing with multiple challenges. When those challenges are adaptive, authority is not enough. The people in the top jobs can't fix what really matters all by themselves, nor can they get to the core of what needs to change without input from you. Clear direction and good management are not enough to bridge The Gap. You have a part to play in whatever happens next.

We also know from our research that when companies and organizations employ a critical mass of people who authorize themselves to lead, they create cultures that value listening, open communication, and collaboration. So although a personal sense of meaning and engagement is terrific, the most important thing you do when you authorize yourself to exercise more leadership is contribute to a culture that is more effective at tackling its toughest problems.

If only a few people in your system see it as their responsibility to exercise leadership, nothing important gets appreciably better. You'll maintain the current (unsatisfying) rate of progress on your adaptive challenges. Your organization will reach uncommon levels of success, however, when more people authorize themselves to exercise leadership on your most important challenge.

MAKING IT REAL

> **Dear Ed and Julia,**
>
> **I've been with my company for three years. We have about 30 employees. I've built up a reputation for hard work and have received one promotion. I always say "yes" with enthusiasm anytime an executive asks for my help. I'm successful with the projects assigned to me, but I crave making more impact. What does it look like for me to lead in this situation?**
>
> **Thanks,**
>
> **—Lizzie Longing to Lead**

Lizzie,

It sounds like you knock the things in your circle out of the park. Well done!

Here's our advice:

1. Get clear on what the biggest challenges facing the company are.

2. Talk about those challenges with others. Ask their opinion. Help them see those challenges.

3. As you learn more about the challenges, look for places where you could (without anyone asking/authorizing you) make a difference. For example, if the company is struggling to connect with younger consumers, write a thought paper on your analysis as to why. Yes, it might be safer to wait until someone higher up asks you to write such a paper, but then again, you are looking for ways to exercise leadership, which, as you know by now, means authorizing yourself.

4. Stepping out of the circle of your authority could attract the attention of someone above you who is looking for more than an enthusiastic "yes." Showing you are a self-starter who can think critically about the future of your company may lead to new opportunities.

13
Start With Your Leadership Challenge

When a friend tells you they are opening a restaurant, a clear image flashes to mind. You've been to restaurants, of course, and you see immediately that your friend will need to hire a chef, create a menu, remodel a building with kitchen and dining areas, and hire servers. You have a mental model. You don't have to think about it.

The same is true for mental models of less concrete ideas. We've had experiences and heard stories, so we understand concepts like sportsmanship, religion, world travel, or new motherhood.

Occasionally, a mental model evolves. Until the early 1900s, for instance, the mental model for a busy street was a downtown corner crowded with horses, carts, and carriages. More abstract mental models evolve too. For thousands of years the mental model of marriage was a legal relationship between a man and a woman. Now, in some cultures, the emerging mental model for marriage is a committed relationship between two people regardless of gender.

We are pushing a new mental model for leadership. In the old model, when someone said the word *leadership,* our minds flashed to one person confidently directing the way forward, telling others what to do to solve their biggest challenges. In other words, our minds flash to a person.

But we now know that the old person-centric model doesn't solve big, hairy 21st century problems.

Put the Challenge at the Center

Rather than *person-centric,* we need to shift to *challengecentric.* We need multiple people, representing different backgrounds and perspectives, to focus their attention on one leadership challenge.

Person-Centric Model	*Challenge-Centric Model*
Leadership is a position.	*Leadership is an activity.*
The person in authority sets the goals and does the leading.	*Everyone is empowered to see and seize their moments to lead.*
Followers focus on and take direction from the "leader."	*Everyone focuses on the same leadership challenge.*

Why Is It Hard to Move Beyond the Person-Centric Model?

Several things make it difficult to put the old person-centric model in our collective rearview mirror:

- **It is baked into our language.** The word *leader* is most often used to reference a person in authority.

- **It serves the interest of those who already have power.** It's a privilege to direct other people. It's fun to have power. That privilege and power can be addictive. For some people in positions of authority, shifting to a challenge-centric model feels like a major loss of control and even status.

- **People in top jobs may not want to admit they don't have the answers.** It's tempting for those in authority to convince themselves (and then others) that because they worked hard to get where they are, they know the best way forward.

- **It is reinforced by most "leadership training."** Most leadership training is designed for a limited number of people who are in or destined for authority roles. The exclusivity of these programs contributes to an assumption that leadership is for the few, not the many.

Most leadership development programs support the old, person-centric model. If you are a participant in one of those trainings, the content (including a battery of personality assessments) is about you. The discussions are about your vision, your strengths, your self-care. The working hypothesis is something like this: You'll be a better leader when you know more about yourself and can use your strengths to motivate other people to tackle the issues you (and sometimes they) care about most.

We are all for knowing thyself and for having a personal vision. Some individuals benefit tremendously from this type of program. But there is more to leadership than that. (And we know plenty of people who are self-aware visionaries yet unable or unwilling to exercise leadership.)

This person-centric model is popular because most of us love talking and learning about ourselves. We've benefited from opportunities offered by these leadership programs to build relationships among an elite group of high achievers. They've also helped us get clear about purpose and our values. This is useful. But there is little evidence that these old-model leadership programs build capacity of their participants to mobilize *others* to make progress on the most important challenges.

Put Your Leadership Challenge at the Center

For 15 years we've pioneered a new model that revolves around a leadership challenge rather than an individual. We ask our participants to describe their leadership challenge in writing before they come to KLC. We offer prompts like these:

- Think about an area of your work or community life in which you aspire to make things better.

- What is the change you want to see? What would success look like?

- What is the background of the problem, opportunity, or challenge?

- Describe the major players, key events, critical past decisions, and so on.

- Why is this leadership challenge important to you?

- What actions have you taken so far?

- What additional actions have you considered?

- In what ways are you stuck or confused?

Over the years we have reviewed more than 10,000 leadership challenges. In our programs, we coach each person to get as clear as possible about their challenge. Knowing *what* the challenge is and *why* progress is important makes it easier to get other people engaged.

Clearly articulating your leadership challenge is similar to planning a trek up a rocky mountain path to enjoy a glorious view. You consider past experiences, pack for weather, map the route and anticipate dangers along the way. You plot the adventure on your smartphone, knowing that when you hit a rough patch, it's the image of the view from the summit that will keep you from giving up and turning around. It's the same thing with challenge-centric leadership. No one would persevere long enough to close The Gap if they didn't have an important purpose and vivid picture of success in mind.

What Happens When We Adopt the Challenge-Centric Model of Leadership?

Five important (and energizing) things happen when we approach a daunting problem this way:

1. **We immediately see why leadership is hard.** As you articulate your challenge and consider questions like, "Who are the major players?" and "Where do you feel stuck?" you'll understand that most of the barriers we described in Part Two are at play with your leadership challenge: There is no quick fix, authority isn't enough, values are involved, and you'll need to energize lots of other people if you want to make lasting change.

2. **We get clear about what progress looks like.** Putting the challenge in the middle changes how we assess attempts at leadership. With the old person-centric model, we judge and second-guess the person out front. With the challenge at the center, we instead evaluate whether the group has made progress. We hold ourselves to as high a standard as anyone else.

3. **We acknowledge the limits of our own authority.** In the old model, if I'm the person out front, it's easy to trick myself into believing I have (or should have) all the power necessary to get people moving in the same direction. Putting the challenge at the center is a great reality check. It becomes easy to see that as the person in authority a big focus of my work needs to be energizing and supporting other people to do their part.

4. **We are more likely to share the load.** Putting the challenge at the center makes us question the mantra "To get it done right, I have to do it myself." When the work is adaptive it doesn't matter how talented or knowledgeable you are. You cannot do all the work. Some of your first acts of leadership will be to understand whether other people care as much about this particular challenge as you do.

5. **We put first things first.** When a challenge anchors our thinking, our priorities change. We define success based on progress on the big challenge rather than on how many things we check off our to-do list.

Your leadership challenge becomes an orienting purpose, a North Star for your leadership efforts. Here are just a few examples of challenges individuals and groups bring to KLC's challenge-centric leadership development programs.

- Administrators from a mid-sized city are focused on the leadership challenge of spurring local job growth through entrepreneurship.

- An equipment leasing company is focused on the leadership challenge of expanding into new territory.

- A director in the department of corrections is focused on the leadership challenge of building credibility for the field so employees enjoy the same respect, pay, and benefits as officers elsewhere in the criminal justice system.

- The executive director of a social service agency is focused on the leadership challenge of eliminating human trafficking in the community.

- An engineer at a manufacturing firm is focused on the leadership challenge of building a cohesive team after a merger combines people from two very different cultures.

- A chamber of commerce focuses on the leadership challenge of redeveloping the downtown to make it more inviting to younger generations.

These situations are different but each challenge is an adaptive one. Each requires leadership from the many, not the few.

Head in the Same Direction, Differently

We close The Gap when enough people put the same leadership challenge at the center of their work. That's a very different approach than the old model that encourages people to fall in step behind one leader on a march toward that person's predetermined goal. Focusing on a common leadership challenge allows everyone to see and seize their moments to lead. While we need a common focus—the leadership challenge—we don't want uniformity or conformity of action. Adaptive work thrives on diversity.

Ed's Aunt Kathleen was a Loretto nun who spent her life in service to others. At her funeral a friend described her this way: "She encouraged us not to conform but inspired us to head in the same direction, differently." Let's ponder that statement for a moment and apply it to our challengecentric model for leadership:

"She encouraged us not to conform . . ." Uniformity won't close The Gap. Conforming to just one approach, or to the wishes of the person in authority, isn't sufficient for progress on our most important challenge.

". . . but inspired us to head in the same direction . . ." To us that means defining the leadership challenge so lots of people can find their unique place in the work. When the orienting direction is broad enough that people can make the purpose personal, they are more likely to heed the call to leadership.

"…differently." Whatever concerns you enough to put at the center is not a simple problem. There is no one solution. Diversity of thought and action is critical.

MAKING IT REAL

Dear Ed and Julia,

I am two months into my new job as president of a community college. I am the fourth person to hold this post in the last three years and have some major issues to deal with. We need to move from distrust and lack of transparency to become nimble, connected, and forward-thinking. We compete for students with other colleges in the region and our retention numbers are dismal. It would be easier if I thought the old model of leadership would work. But it won't! Your challenge-centric leadership model gives me hope that I can work with college trustees and my executive team to turn things around. But I have to admit, I don't know where to start. Help!

—Gabriela Got the Job (and Now I Have to Deliver)

Gabriela,

You said it: The challenge at the center is student retention. That is a purpose big, broad, and important enough for everyone—from college trustees to first-year faculty—to find their unique moments to experiment and exercise leadership.

Naming the leadership challenge and focusing attention on it is your work as the senior authority. As you listen to other people's concerns and aspirations, don't hesitate to tell them that, for you, the most important challenge is student retention. You need enough of your college focusing their leadership efforts on that challenge.

Keep student retention in the middle of your thinking. Anchor it in your meetings and discussions. Make it clear that your leadership, and the leadership of others, will be evaluated against progress on this challenge.

14
Start Where You Have Influence

When thinking about tough problems we often focus on what those people over there, behind that tree or in the next building, need to do. We let our own people (the people who think like us, value what we value, and have the same general orientation to the problem that we do) off the hook.

Progress on our most important challenges will require some of us to engage with people we don't know and who have very different experiences and backgrounds than we do. But most of us can influence progress by leading within our existing sphere of influence: among our friends, peers, and colleagues.

Anyone can lead, although leadership might look different coming from different people.

Our colleague Kaye Monk-Morgan was skeptical at first about the principle "anyone can lead, anytime, anywhere." Though Kaye had been trained in our framework and was using many of its tools in her work as a university administrator, she had convinced herself that as the youngest person on the executive team and the only Black woman, she had little influence over their decisions and no ability to exercise leadership.

But, she was (and still is!) passionate about the university's mission and especially about students who, like her, were the first in their family to go to college. She felt she didn't have influence with the whole team but was called to do something, to share her insights and alternative perspectives somehow. She took the initiative to engage with her supervisor privately about what she was feeling and found he agreed with her assessment of what was happening. They agreed to partner to make sure her ideas got airtime, and he started making a practice of amplifying her contributions in meetings where, unsurprisingly, they swiftly gained traction with the rest of the team.

Still, Kaye had a hard time calling what she was doing *leadership*. Only after her mother weighed in did Kaye's own take on leadership, as an activity available to everyone, including a Black woman on an otherwise all-white and mostly male executive team, begin to shift.

"Honey," Kaye's mom told her as they talked on the phone, debriefing after yet another draining day at work, "You were looking for leadership in one particular way. No one told you how it was going to show up. You were able to provoke your supervisor to do something different as a result of your request. How is that not leadership?"

If You Don't Have the Title, You Can Still Use Your Influence

Accepting that leadership is about seeing and seizing moments to mobilize others is a massive paradigm shift for most people. It democratizes leadership, making it available to the many rather than the select few. It breaks down the mythology of a "great leader," and replaces it with an accessible framework for making progress on important challenges.

Here are a few examples:

- A once-proud entrepreneurial company has lost its mojo. Innovation is rare and the CEO is distracted, but the middle manager can still do her part by creating an entrepreneurial culture in her department. She doesn't have authority over everything, but she does over some things.

- Partisan gridlock may have overtaken the nation, but an individual can still reach out to someone in his community who regularly votes the ticket of the other party. The two can decide to swap stories and look for common values.

- Despite staff training and all-school assemblies organized by the principal, a middle school still experiences more and more bullying. A young student can't influence everything in the school, but they can speak up when one of their friends mistreats a classmate.

- A bank teller who wants to keep the local branch open in a low-income neighborhood can imagine three different explanations for why there are fewer walk-in customers at the branch than there were 12 months ago. Then, she can share her observations and possible explanations with her supervisor and ask if they have noticed anything similar.

- The middle manager at a global company, lost in the sea of middle managers and passionate about his company's efforts to overcome a lack of inclusion and diversity, can make a point of talking with his work friends who have various perspectives on the issue. He can quietly prepare for a conversation with his supervisor and, hopefully, after that, his team.

Historically, our favorite example of "start where you have influence" is Rosa Parks who, in Montgomery, Alabama, in 1955, refused to give her bus seat to a white passenger. Her influence fueled a civil rights movement and led to the Voting Rights Act of 1965. Rosa Parks understood that everyone—even those with no formal authority or position—has the responsibility to seize their moment to lead.

No One Leads Everywhere, So We Need Everyone Leading Somewhere

You might not be able to do everything, but you can do something. And here's the thing about deep, daunting, adaptive challenges: No one can do all the leading themselves. No one's sphere of influence can reach everyone. Adaptive challenges aren't solved by one person and certainly not just by the person in authority. Big, complex challenges—the really important ones—get solved when enough people step up, take risks, and exercise leadership.

It's tempting to hear "lead where you have influence" as a rallying call for those lower on an org chart. It's more than that. Those in key authority positions bemoan the limits of their influence too. They are also frustrated about their inability, when the challenge is adaptive, to get everyone moving in the same direction.

For example, the leadership challenge for a CEO of a large company might be to create a more inclusive culture. She can do a lot to seed the ground—including bringing in speakers on the topic, modeling inclusive behaviors, prioritizing discussions about inclusion—but she can't expect training, modeling, and messages from her alone to be enough to solve the problem. She needs people at all levels engaged around the adaptive challenge. She focuses her influence where it will be most powerful—perhaps with her direct reports. But she needs them to take up the cause in their spheres of influence too. The goal is people in overlapping spheres of influence modeling more inclusion in various parts of the company and holding one another accountable for progress in ways the CEO alone could never do.

The influence of elected officials is similarly limited. The minority leader of a state's house of representatives has lots of influence on house members in their own party but little to none on those whose allegiances lie elsewhere. Even elected officials at the very top of their political hierarchy, such as a president, prime minister, or governor, have limited influence. Leading within their sphere of influence and partnering with those with other spheres of influence is key.

The Temptation to Lead Outside Your Influence

There may be a time or a place when you decide it is worth the effort to try to exercise leadership beyond your sphere of influence. For example:

- A politician attempts to rally support from the opposition in the waning hours before a key vote.

- A young professional intervenes with senior management, hoping to swing their decision on a key matter.

- A student speaks before the school board urging a more comprehensive approach to stop bullying in the district.

But it's a massive undertaking to mobilize those outside your influence. If that politician, young professional, and student succeed in drawing new and sustained attention to their challenges, we would describe their efforts as leadership. Typically, though, major change occurs because enough people, in different spheres, lead where they have influence.

To exercise leadership, you have to capture attention. Getting that attention from those who already connect with or respect you is easier than drawing strangers or even opponents to your priorities. If it's important to draw in strangers or opponents, that message needs to come from someone they know and trust, not from you.

Leading Where You Have Influence Gets Results

Here are six reasons to start leading where you have influence (and to coach those you influence to do the same):

1. **The people in your sphere of influence are part of the problem.** They have a part, at least a small part, in why the problem you are working on exists, and therefore they need to play a part in solving it. (See the following chapter for more.)

2. **You can get started right away.** You already have their attention. You may meet with them regularly or see them over lunch every day. If you start asking their opinion or inviting their ideas, they are highly likely to engage.

3. **You'll have more success.** Leadership is always hard, but it's easier when you are intervening with people who already have an affinity for you and sympathy for your cause.

4. **You'll mobilize change.** It might not be sufficient to get the ultimate progress you are after, but it's something. It's a start and a piece you can uniquely contribute.

5. **You'll model taking responsibility.** Your example might inspire someone else to do the same, unleashing a leadership contagion in your group, team, organization, or community.

6. **You'll practice and get better at leading.** If you dream of exercising leadership in bigger and bigger ways, you should practice seizing the moments you have.

Leadership is always risky and the biggest risk is disappointing your own people. The fear of doing so leads us to think that leadership is getting those other people—in the other department, in the other political party, in the other faction—to do something different. When that's our orientation, it's easy to beat up on the other, to feel self-righteous about it, and to receive praise and adulation from our people for it, all the while not really risking much of anything.

A heroic individual confronting the opposition makes a nice leadership story, but it's rarely how the toughest problems get seen and solved. When everyone leads—when everyone is pushing, pulling, and cajoling their own people to change—is when we make progress on our toughest challenges. Progress on adaptive challenge requires leadership that is widely distributed. The more people start leading within their circles of influence, the more factions become activated, the more people seize their moments, and the faster tough problems get solved.

MAKING IT REAL

Dear Ed and Julia,

My leadership challenge is climate change. I recognize the losses people have to deal with if we are going to save ourselves from extinction, so I try to stay patient with people who aren't willing to do simple things like bring reusable bags to the grocery store. But I'm afraid for the future! There are so many people who think this is a nonissue. How do I get them to listen and change their behavior?

—Sal Wants to Seize the Moment

Dear Sal,

You are out front on a cause that masses of people would rather not think about. Ask yourself, "Do I want to be right or do I want to be effective?" You didn't say that people are getting tired of your rants, but we have to wonder. Instead of trying to change people who think this is a nonissue, start with lower-hanging fruit. Focus on people who acknowledge the issue but need help changing their habits. Look for partners who will share the work and keep you hopeful. Stay patient and keep the challenge at the center. Momentum on our toughest problems builds one sphere of influence at a time.

15

Start With Your Part of the Mess

Our biggest, most important challenges are cocreated. We all own part of the mess and we each need to deal with our part.

One political faction doesn't polarize a society all by itself. And your emotionally distant sibling didn't get that far removed from the family circle all on her own. Multiple factors and many people contributed to creating these deep-rooted problems in the first place. A complex, adaptive challenge will always resist the simple approach of blaming other people and thinking they need to solve it on their own.

Sales numbers don't decline year after year just because the marketing department is dysfunctional. Perhaps manufacturing happily assumes the product line doesn't need to change. Maybe the CEO is congratulating himself for acting quickly to fix the problem ("I replaced the head of marketing!") and thinking that's all that should be necessary to send sales upward. Maybe everyone else is going about their business secure in the belief that improving sales is somebody else's job.

"You know, I should have taken the bypass."

But if the challenge is adaptive, blaming one person or department (or one political faction, or one racial group) is a recipe for long-term disaster.

Start With the One Person You Can Control

When scientists run experiments, they change an independent variable to see if the dependent variable changes. With leadership on a tough challenge, the simplest variable to change is you. Frustrated with what others are doing? Change something about the way you behave and see what happens. If you see a problem in your community and focus only on what other people should be doing differently, you miss a golden opportunity to see and seize your moments to lead.

Here are some examples of people who've had the courage to identify their part of the mess:

- A state representative abhors the current level of political partisanship and polarization. While he can't change the entire system, he can at least decide not to use inflammatory language about the other side in his speeches and public remarks. He can watch how people respond as he shifts his language. Then, he can share what he learns with constituents and colleagues and encourage them to own their part of the mess.

- An old company acquires a new start-up, doubling the number of employees. Significant culture issues emerge in the combined company. The old company had lots of complex processes and a hierarchical structure. The employees from the new start-up are used to a more engaging, free-wheeling culture with a flat structure. Higher-ups have said that "forming one, new culture" should be the challenge for every employee and team. Instead of thinking she's too insignificant to make a difference, a front-line employee with the original company realizes the way she approaches her work is reinforcing two cultures. She hears herself scolding new colleagues when they don't respect hierarchy, trying to get them to adapt to her culture. So she starts experimenting with new ways of engaging, following the lead of some of her new colleagues from the acquired company, hoping it sparks a blend of cultures in at least her part of the company.

- A priest longs for his parish to unite in its efforts to slow a pandemic. Two clear factions have emerged in the congregation, one wanting to promote masking and vaccines and the other encouraging members to resist those public health efforts. The priest realizes that while forging unity will take time and a change of heart by many, he can start a regular joint coffee date with the most vocal people in each faction as a way to create understanding, at least on a small scale.

Consider Your Immunity to Change

With their groundbreaking book *Immunity to Change,* Bob Kegan and Lisa Lahey help millions of people pinpoint their part of the mess. The book and their workshops coax individuals and teams to see how sometimes our own habits and mindsets are the biggest barriers to the change we want to see in the world.

Kegan and Lahey help readers understand that often, as you complain about your current reality on the one hand (i.e., "I'm not getting promoted," "Our organization isn't growing," etc.), you actually contribute to that reality on the other. A manager might shrink from expressing interest in moving up because she's scared to shoulder more responsibility. Or an executive team may be so intensely loyal to their current strategies that they refuse to lean into new strategies that might propel more growth.

Kegan and Lahey describe the ways in which long-standing habits and unexamined insecurities keep us stuck in the status quo. They call this having one foot on the gas and the other on the brake. Participants in *Immunity to Change* workshops create maps to reveal the unique ways in which a foot on the brake is holding them back—individually or as a team—from achieving a big change goal.

When we face and fix our part of the mess, we take our foot off the brake. If you take a look at your part of the problem, you unlock your part of the solution as well.

Why Is It So Hard to Start With Your Part of the Mess?

There are plenty of understandable reasons people fail to see how they've contributed to the current reality. You may recognize a few of these:

- **We jealously guard our self-image.** Few of us go to bed at night, lay our head on the pillow, and reflect on all the trouble we've caused. We'd rather think of ourselves as the hero, or at least as a silent actor, but certainly not as a contributor to the problem.

- **We surround ourselves with people who think like us.** So many of us spend our workdays and leisure time with people who share our worldview. These people likely have similar opinions and don't call attention to our blind spots. If everyone you interact with thinks the challenge you are facing is the marketing department's fault, or the Republicans' fault, or the Democrats' fault, you aren't likely to decide that some of it is *your* fault.

- **We want to believe there really is a simple solution to our most important challenges.** We want to believe that if this person or that group changes their approach, everything will solve itself. Or if one person left the company everything would right itself. We keep believing long after it's clear that there is no quick fix.

- **We have our go-to moves and we want to use them.** Often our part of the mess is thinking that we can make progress without getting out of our comfort zone. It's difficult to realize your go-to moves won't be enough.

- **We have people depending on us to bring home a paycheck.** We worry that if we admit our part of the mess, or even admit that we are stuck we'll be judged insufficient. We are afraid to lose our reputation or our job. We decide it's best to put our heads down and just plug away at the day-to-day stuff.

A Timeless Secret to Progress

Of course, we didn't invent the "what's your part of the mess" idea:

- Mahatma Gandhi exhorted us to be the change we want to see in the world. He told followers, "If we could change ourselves, the tendencies of the world would also change. . . . We need not wait to see what others do."

- And in the Bible's Book of Matthew, Jesus asks, "Why do you look at the speck of sawdust in your brother's eye and pay no attention to the plank in your own eye?"

- Centuries before that in the Talmud, the central text of Rabbinic Judaism, Rabbi Hillel asked his students, "If I am only for myself then what am I? And if not now, when?"

When we explore our part of the mess, humility and curiosity soften our hearts and open our minds toward other people. That leads to a better diagnosis of the situation and to more purposeful and effective action.

Get Everyone Asking, "What's My Part of This Mess?"

One person can see a problem, get more curious about it, and use their influence to make things better. But real change begins when lots of people get curious about what's really going on with a problem or challenge.

Every time someone authentically asks themselves "What's my part of the mess?"—and pauses long enough to hear the answer—they generate the possibility of their own leadership, marshaling the one variable they can control. Progress is usually just around the corner.

MAKING IT REAL

Dear Ed and Julia,

Hi!

I'm intrigued by this idea of starting with my part of the mess. I'm a spiritual person so, big picture, it's not hard to admit. But I need some help making it specific. I'm a high school teacher and our principal appointed me co-chair of a big school-wide redesign effort. The purpose of our redesign is to transform the educational experience and teach students the habits of success they will need throughout high school and beyond.

We launched tons of new curricular resources and innovative class schedule options. But teachers need to take ownership, and right now they aren't. It's so frustrating! We could be on the cutting edge if they would just step up! I know everything we've rolled out can be overwhelming, but still . . .

This is going to work through trial and error, problemsolving, collaborating, sharing, and reflecting. That's how we'll evolve our culture of learning! I want to make a difference in the lives of my students, colleagues, and community. If I really am part of this mess, I want to know about it! Help please!

—Adrian Accepts Feedback Please!!!

Dear Adrian,

Your greatest strengths may be your greatest weakness and also the place to start looking for your part of the mess. Surely your principal tapped you to co-chair this giant effort because you are enthusiastic, optimistic, and committed to student learning above all else. But other teachers may not be so receptive to your drive for change. Perhaps they see things differently, or have other issues weighing on them—personal, professional, or even historical—that may make it hard for them to tolerate the uncertainty that comes with change.

Have you paused your drive forward long enough to really listen one on one to your fellow teachers? Your part of the mess may be (and we certainly don't know for sure) a failure to see each of them as individuals with their own lived experience and, perhaps, well-founded fears and insecurities. If you slow down, acknowledge you've left some people behind, and start to ask more open-hearted questions, you may be surprised by the results. And don't be afraid to apologize for the role you've played in creating the sense of overwhelm. As you admit your part of the mess, we bet they'll start to acknowledge theirs.

Stay strong. The school is lucky to have you.

16
Start Engaging Others

One of two things tends to happen when we begin work on an adaptive challenge: We either attempt to go it alone (the hero coming in to save the day) or we bring in like-minded colleagues (who bring the same limited perspective on the problem and possible solutions as we do). The first approach prioritizes our ego, the second our comfort. Neither works.

The temptation to toil away at the work by yourself or with your closest allies is alluring. This can be especially true if you lack confidence in your ability to contribute. On the other hand, if you've made a good career out of being an expert or an authority, you may be more comfortable creating plans and delivering answers than you are at trusting that you will have more of an impact when you engage others.

Going It Alone Doesn't Work

Going it alone may be your habit or your preference, but it doesn't work. Even the most brilliant person's knowledge and wits will never be enough to solve the biggest challenges facing companies and communities. If the situation you are facing is an adaptive challenge, tackling it by yourself won't work. Instead, you need more people (ideally everyone in your system) willing and ready to experiment and exercise leadership.

With technical problems a smart person can work on their own and get the job done. A mechanic is the right person to toil away under the hood to fix your car. Focus groups and stakeholder engagement won't help that mechanic fix the car faster or better. Bringing your whole family to the repair shop to provide their perspective on the problem would bea total waste of time. The same is true for technical work at the office or in your volunteer life. But it's a different story when the work is adaptive. With more complex challenges you need other people.

Ed learned this lesson the hard way when he served in his state's house of representatives. He had great success oneyear working with a bipartisan group of legislators to forge a solution to a highly divisive issue about school funding. Engagement with stakeholders and other legislators was high, resulting in a growing, diverse group embracing a collective way forward. But the next year he took a different approach on a similarly divisive challenge. Despite his earlier success, this time Ed went it alone. He should have engaged diverse voices and sought partnership, input, and collective learning, but instead he toiled away crafting a "perfect" plan. When he finally presented the plan to others, the reception was lukewarm. A year before, Ed engaged others and had success. When he went solo the following year, he had little to show for his work.

Sticking Close to Like-Minded Colleagues Doesn't Work Either

Upon hearing advice like "don't go it alone" and "engage other people," a common first impulse is to bring in your go-to crew.

But you won't make progress on adaptive challenges by engaging only with people who share your perspective. We find comfort in people who think like us, but they often reinforce our preconceived notions. We need an open mind for adaptive work.

Look no further than America's dysfunctional politics to understand this dynamic. In the 1990s and early 2000s progressives and conservatives began to seek out media outlets that reinforced their political views. Now that dynamic has spread to what neighborhood you live in or what faith community you attend. It even shows up in where you shop (progressives at Target, conservatives at Walmart) and your preferred brands (Subaru, Lu Lu Lemon and Starbucks for progressives; Chevy, Duluth Trading Company and Dunkin' for conservatives). We are oversimplifying here, of course, but it's impossible not to see the trends. As Americans, we are sorting ourselves more and more into groups with like-minded preferences and perspectives and cutting off options of finding a middle ground.

Julia has scars related to this lesson. She was elected to the local school board in her small, rural community. All seven members of the board identified a new $28 million campus as the way to keep their schools vibrant and attractive. A series of promotional sessions masquerading as community input occurred. Then the board put the tax issue (needed to fund the $28 million) up for vote in the community. The measure lost with only 197 votes for the new school and 929 against.

Julia had lived in rural America for only a few years. She discovered the level of debt the board was asking taxpayers to shoulder was not only difficult for the vast majority to manage, but wildly incongruent with rural values of frugality and preservation.

Julia realized she had been in an echo chamber of likemindedness. Instead of giving up, the board learned from its failure. They started engaging others, as they should have been doing all along. They brought diverse perspectives together and authorized a representative task force to recommend a new way forward. After months of listening and leadership, task force members recommended a middle ground. Their trust in the process restored, voters approved a smaller, but still significant $12 million renovation of the two existing school buildings.

Abandon the Echo Chamber of the Like-Minded

It isn't only folks in civic and political life who fall into the trap that Julia and the school board did before the first vote. People in organizations and companies are all too willing to enjoy their own echo chambers of the like-minded. Salespeople associate most with salespeople, back-office people with back-office people, executives with fellow executives, young professionals with young professionals.

But in adaptive work there is no clear way forward. The sooner you expand the circle of people bringing their perspectives to the same challenge, the better.

Because there are many ways to look at a problem or challenge, engaging others—especially those who have different perspectives and share different values—illuminates the situation. You begin to see the problem more completely and together you can devise solutions that are more comprehensive.

Likewise, by engaging those who think differently than you about a particular challenge, you help ensure they aren't, consciously or unconsciously, working against you.

What Makes It Hard to Engage Others?

It's rare to experience robust, effective engagement. These things can get in the way:

- **Our typical approaches to engagement are often insufficient.** For example, *engagement* for governing bodies usually means a public comment period during a city council or school board meeting. Typically, this means individuals take turns speaking from behind a podium. Often there is no or little interaction between the speaker and the governing body or the audience. Speakers are usually limited to a set amount of time, such as five minutes. We are in favor of public engagement with the government, but this standard approach becomes mere political theater when people are trying to address daunting challenges.

- **We sometimes fail to acknowledge disparities that make it difficult for people to engage.** Often, especially in the nonprofit and civic sectors, we say we want to hear from diverse voices, but we don't do enough to eliminate barriers to engagement. Do the people we say we want to hear from have transportation and child care to allow them to attend a meeting? Are they being compensated for their time in equitable ways? Are we willing to be influenced by disruptive ideas or are we including diverse voices just so we can check a box?

- **We may lack the imagination to create new structures and processes for engagement.** The standard public comment process in governing bodies is the only process we've experienced. The all-staff meeting in our company is all we know. We just keep replicating what we've done without imagining how those processes are serving us (or not!).

MAKING IT REAL

> **Dear Ed and Julia,**
>
> I am pretty high up at a state natural resource conservation agency. The challenge I care most about right now is creating an inclusive park system where people of color feel welcome to visit, enjoy the parks, and become engaged with conserving our public land. My question is, when should we engage representatives from those communities? Is it really fair to expect them to exercise leadership on this issue when they have challenges of their own?
>
> **—Casey the Cautious Conservationist**

Dear Casey,

We can't presume to say what challenges should become priorities for anyone else. But you will be more successful if you engage from the start the communities you hope will become more frequent visitors to and defenders of public parks. Some people or groups you invite to engage with this challenge may focus their efforts elsewhere. That's fine. Trust people to make those choices on their own.

Use your convening power to engage the right people from the start. Support people in being authentic, even provocative, in their feedback and challenging in their requests of you and your agency. You are attempting to shift a system with deeply entrenched norms and patterns and to engage people who may not have felt welcomed or included before. Be patient and find your allies. It will be worth it.

Part Four

Use the Heat

We've explored the connection between our toughest challenges and things like loss, risk, disturbance, and conflict. At KLC we often use the word *heat* as shorthand for those things. Progress on adaptive challenges requires facing that heat. Notice we say *facing*, not *eliminating*. In Part Four we explore how and why heat is necessary for progress.

Think of your organization as a skillet. Exercising leadership involves taking the temperature and regulating the flame—doing everything you can to keep the oil bubbling at just the right temperature for change. If the heat is too low around an important challenge, not enough people get engaged and understand the need for change. On the other hand, if the heat around your challenge is too high, a fight or flight response kicks in. Tensions escalate and conflict disrupts all attempts at forward motion.

To solve the really tough challenges, we need to find a middle place from which people who see a problem differently can all recognize the challenge and feel the freedom to contribute, ask questions, and experiment with solutions. We need to create spaces and facilitate conversations in which the temperature around an important issue is neither too hot nor too cold. Leadership involves stepping in to make sure no important stakeholders get so burned that they abandon the work, even as you allow new perspectives to pop up, like perfect kernels of corn. We need lots of people, throughout your system, exercising leadership to generate and maintain productive levels of heat long enough to reach your aspirations for change.

As you've certainly seen for yourself, one person cannot regulate the heat by themselves. Everyone needs to be able to take the temperature and be willing to put their hand on the dial, seizing moments to lower the flame if conflict rises and the group risks losing important voices. Likewise, all of us have to be poised to turn the heat up if our most important challenge starts slipping to the sidelines of collective attention.

People with authority have significant, even essential, things they can do to regulate heat. But keeping the focus on the challenge is not their work alone. None of us gets to stand aside thinking, "There is nothing I can do to contribute to progress here." Wherever you sit in relation to the challenge, you will be able to try something to get things popping. When it comes to keeping people in the *productive zone*, we all have a part to play.

17

Work Avoidance: When the Heat Is Too Low

For most individuals and organizations, The Gap-revealing questions from Part One of this book ("When you think about the future of your organization, what concerns you the most?" and "What is your greatest aspiration?") elicit answers about concerns and aspirations people have been carrying around for years. A company is perpetually concerned about employee engagement. A nonprofit board's biggest aspiration is equitable educational opportunities for all young people. A regional economic council is more concerned about brain drain with each passing decade.

What's going on? Why is it so hard for us to make progress on the things we say are most important? One answer is *work avoidance*.

Few of us feel responsible for keeping the heat around an issue high enough for long enough for real change to happen. It's as if we are putting oil and popcorn in the skillet and then every once in a while, we send one person over to flip on the flame for

"It's only grown that one tooth so far, so I don't know what you are worried about."

a few seconds. Our most important challenges persist because most of us are really good at avoiding the sustained, collective work required to make progress on entrenched, adaptive challenges.

We Avoid Adaptive Work Because It's Uncomfortable

As much as we say we want to solve our toughest challenges, we avoid difficult work because it gets in the way of other things we desire. We want a casual, friendly atmosphere at work, so we don't raise the issues that will make people uncomfortable. We want to be liked, so we resist offering ideas counter to the group norm. We want to be thought of as competent, or oneof the gang, so we don't challenge prevailing wisdom or suggest alternatives to "the way we do things around here." We hold ourselves back from sharing provocative data or asking obvious questions for fear of being labeled a troublemaker and being passed over for the next great project or promotion.

Here's a silly example, albeit not necessarily an adaptive one: Ed hated mowing the yard when he was a kid. He put it off until the grass was embarrassingly tall. Even then, rather than getting started right away, he would first change the battery in his headphones and spend time deciding what music to listen to while mowing. Then he would go to the gas station to fill up the gas tank, even though the mower already had enough gas. He might sketch a new mowing route, trying to decipher the most efficient path across the yard. Of course, those activities were just delaying and avoiding the real work of mowing!

We do things like this in our grown-up lives too.

Here are a few examples:

- A city council wrestling with the perennially difficult issue of homelessness appoints yet another task force to study it. The recommendations of past task forces remain on the shelf, not implemented.

- A corporate team needs a tough discussion about the performance of one of its units. That discussion is last onthe agenda for the weekly meeting. Everyone knows the discussion is vital. But most of the meeting is spent discussing miscellaneous topics. With three minutes left in the meeting, the team turns its attention to the performance issue. Rushed and with nowhere near enough time to surface the tough stuff, they rehash complaints and leave the meeting, having ticked a few, mostly procedural things off their list but having let the big and adaptive problem fester.

- Yet another round of strategic planning could be work avoidance too. It is easier to imagine all the things that should and could be done in the future rather than do what's needed now.

Low heat looks like people going through the motions, taking their normal approaches, attempting to solve the problem the way they've always attempted to solve problems. In each of those examples well-meaning people take action that keeps the heat around a tough challenge too low. Their actions (the task force, the three-minute discussion, the strategic plan) inadvertently impede progress by allowing the group to once again go through the motions rather than address deeper, more significant questions.

Why We Engage in Work Avoidance

Progress on tough, adaptive challenges requires us to stay at it when the heat gets high. But that can be hard. It doesn't come naturally to most of us. It's easier to avoid that work because:

- **We recognize there will be loss.** Progress on adaptive challenges is evolutionary. We need to let go of something to move forward. But we are hardwired to resist letting go of things we value. We avoid difficult work when we perceive that work means we must let go of prized valuesor change relationships with people we care about.

- **We hate discomfort.** Addressing a tough issue raises the heat, and more heat means more discomfort. "If I misjudge the situation and raise the heat too quickly, I might be the kernel that gets burned."

- **It's easy to convince ourselves we've done enough.** Too often we give up after one effort to solve the challenge, satisfied with ourselves, thinking, "At least I tried."

- **We are not sure the problem can ever be solved.** Some problems—like homelessness, poverty, and climate change— seem so big that one person, team, organization, or community can never make a dent in the issue. So we throw up our hands and miss opportunities to make a difference.

- **We want to keep people happy.** People in authority are particularly susceptible to this type of work avoidance. They've been hired (or elected or appointed) to set the vision and direct the way forward. Others look to them for order and security. They are expected to fix problems. The temptation for them, then, is to treat every challenge as something to be solved quickly or avoided, pushed along, or pushed aside. This keeps people happy in the short-term but allows adaptive issues to fester.

How We Engage in Work Avoidance

Three ways stand out:

1. **We push the adaptive challenge off to someone else or some other time.** A government appoints a task force to study the issue and report back. A global firm hires a director of diversity, equity, and inclusion while the executive team attends to business as usual and rarely discusses how to be more inclusive.

2. **We do something (almost anything) to look busy and appear as if we are addressing the problem.** A company restructures its org chart and hopes for better results. An advocacy group gets hundreds of people out for an impromptu protest but fails to anticipate ways to keep those people engaged beyond one Saturday morning march. A group takes up lots of time discussing mundane questions, leaving the big questions, with no easy answers, unasked and unattended.

3. We blame or shame anyone who dares to say something about a tough problem. The boss lashes out at her direct report for bringing bad news, thus attacking the messenger, leaving the message unheeded, and allowing the challenge to become more entrenched.

The more people who are ready to lead, the harder it is for groups to engage in work avoidance. And once we, collectively, say "no" to work avoidance, we are more willing and ready to raise the heat.

MAKING IT REAL

Dear Ed and Julia,

Everywhere I go I see people avoiding the hard work. In our government, in my job, in my volunteer board work, even in my family. It's nothing but avoid, avoid, avoid. I exercise, meditate, and probably drink too much, all to keep from thinking about the dire state of everything.

—Halle Is Helpless and Verging on Despair

Dear Halle,

You are not helpless and if you are drinking too much or deeply depressed, schedule a meeting with a counselor right away. If that was an exaggeration, recognize that giving into despair is a form of *work avoidance*!

Refocus the energy you seem to spend ruminating on all that is bad in the world and use it to start experimenting in just one area of your life. Your volunteer board could be a good place to practice since the risks of exercising leadership may be lower there than in the workplace. Remember, articulating the challenge at the center of your work is a great first step. Name it. Write it down. Then, go back to The Gap exercise in Chapter 5. Start asking friends and fellow board members what concerns them the most about the situation you've elevated.

While you'll eventually need to help more people gain courage to stop avoiding the work, for now just remember, leadership starts with you.

18

Tempers Flare: When the Heat Is Too High

The last chapter explored what happens when the heat around a tough challenge stays too low. This chapter goes the opposite direction. When the heat is too high, productive work is impossible. Rather than work through differences to generate understanding and progress, a group lets unproductive conflict reign.

Let's revisit our popcorn analogy. When the oil starts smoking the heat is too high for popping. If you don't turn it down quickly, you end up with charred kernels and a smoked-up kitchen that smells bad for days. We are seeing a lot of smoky kitchens lately.

When Ed and Julia started working together back in 2009 we rarely found ourselves coaching and advising peopleto turn down the heat. In the early 2000s someone exercising leadership usually needed to find more moments to raise the heat. While that's still crucial, it's getting increasingly important to know when and how to lower the heat.

When the heat gets too high, not only do we not get progress on the challenge, we also risk losing community or company cohesion. To protect themselves, people turn firmly away from one another, or they become angry versions of themselves, attacking others and burning bridges.

It's not that we long for the good old days of greater civility in our public discourse. Those days never really existed. Too many people and communities waited centuries for their voices to be heard and their aspirations to influence the policies and practices of governments and institutions. The higher heat around race and equity issues, for instance, may be a sign that things are finally changing in meaningful and lasting ways.

But the heat around a tough issue is only useful if it illuminates moments for leadership and progress instead of burning through relationships and destroying opportunities for positive change.

Many factors contribute to making the process of seeking common ground—especially in civic life—harder, morevolatile, and less productive. Maybe in the future, cultural anthropologists will trace this phenomenon to the rise of social media and the decline of real relationships with our neighbors. But what we know from our own experience is that the temperature around important issues is getting hotter and hotter. To use another metaphor, society is a pressure cooker and we are always just one degree away from the lid blowing off.

When the Lid Blows Off

A large city recently engaged our team to facilitate community engagement around a proposed nondiscrimination ordinance. The rhetoric up to that point had been inflammatory and accusatory. The predominant factions were the LGBTQ community on one side, advocating for more protections, especially for transgender people, and conservative faith communities on the other, who were advocating for religious liberty. The testimony from members of the public during city council meetings largely reflected national talking points from those two factions. Meanwhile, despite months of debate, key questions about what the ordinance would and would not allow remained unexplored and unanswered.

Observers worried that escalating public tension would damage how the community functioned for years to come.

People were talking past one another, factions were digging in, and no one was listening to anyone else. Although many people had substantive questions about what the ordinance would or would not do, up until the point we came on board, a forum hadn't been found in which to explore them. The local media seemed more interested in covering the controversy around the proposed ordinance than describing what was in the ordinance and how it would interface with state and federal nondiscrimination laws. Every article and online post only served to increase the temperature and fuel divides.

We knew from past experience that one way to lower heat is to have competing factions work together to address some small, but crucial aspect of the problem. We hosted two evening meetings using a facilitated process to help key stakeholders, no matter their position on the proposed ordinance, explore what was in the proposal and how, if passed, it would change things for individuals, employers, landlords, schools, public businesses, and religious institutions.

In this case, getting into the weeds of a legal document in which everyone had a vested interest helped lower the heat. As the process unfolded, the two opposing sides began to engage differently with one another and the proposed ordinance. It helped to have the full range of stakeholders in the room, including some, such as advocates for veterans and people with disabilities and representatives from the NAACP, who hadn't been heard from much in the council's public comment periods.

Opponents came to understand that most of the protections in the proposed local ordinance already existed at state and federal levels. Although they still opposed the ordinance, their opposition tempered as they began to more fully understand how little new ground was being plowed.

Likewise, proponents became more measured and tempered with their enthusiasm. They began speaking more directly about details and parts of the ordinance, rather than reverting to the broad national rhetoric.

The heat came down and for a few moments on the second night, people from the two most polarized factions asked curious questions of one another and listened with genuine empathy. Later, the city council revised the ordinance to include some of the groups' suggested improvements. Ultimately, the ordinance passed. Plenty of people remained opposed on economic, political, or moral grounds, but the tenor of the debate had changed. By engaging in a process that lowered the heat, this group of people with conflicting values, perspectives, and preferences around a divisive issue became less hostile and more productive in their discourse.

The Heat's Too High

Although our example of facilitating productive work around the nondiscrimination ordinance springs from civic life, blow-ups happen everywhere these days. People are on edge. The right amount of heat overcomes work avoidance and provokes learning and progress, but too much heat cuts off productive dialogue. People can't listen and it becomes impossible to discover new ways forward together.

Learn the Signs of a System Ready to Explode

Watch for these indications that the temperature around a tough challenge is headed up past the point of productivity:

- **A fight, flight, or freeze response kicks in.** Whenever anyone mentions the tough challenge, a few people lean in and prepare to do battle, some check out, and others get overloaded and are unable to respond. This might present as a few voices becoming strained and louder, while most people either shut down completely or get up and leave the room.

- **People argue past one another.** No one is listening. No one is asking questions. Conversation becomes a volley of rhetorical bombs designed to upset or box in the other side.

- **Interventions play to one faction while alienating another.** Each argument and every action seems designed to rally people on one side of the issue and upset people on the other. No one makes a move to open up possibilities and seek common ground.

- **People aren't learning anything.** Curiosity and learning are key to solving adaptive challenges. When learning stops, opportunities for leadership evaporate.

- **People demonize one another.** Rather than seeking to understand, those involved seek to blame the problem (and often a cascade of other evils) on one person, one team, one department, or one malevolent outside force.

Brain scientists tell us, and most of us know from experience, that high-stress situations provoke predictable patterns of psychological responses in one of two categories: When tensions escalate some people get hyper-aroused, agitated, and even explosive. Others disassociate, becoming depressed, withdrawn, almost frozen. When the heat around a challenge becomes so high that it activates these kinds of stress responses, people can't learn, they can't engage productively around conflict, and they can't find ways to compromise. Leadership, in those situations, means finding ways to lower the heat.

How Everyone Leading Keeps the Heat From Getting Too High

Anyone can exercise leadership to help keep the heat in check and a situation from exploding. Consider this:

- **Managing self is a leadership behavior.** The more people in your organization or community that can manage themselves—that is, stay calm in the face of adversity, channel their emotions, and choose more strategic reactions—the more likely it is that you will be able to keep the heat productive. One of the reasons that our intervention around the nondiscrimination ordinance worked was that stakeholders worked hard to manage themselves; for the most part, they gained credibility each time they spoke up rather than, as had been the case during the city council meetings, provoking outrage from the other side.

- **Helping a group stick to purpose is a leadership behavior.** The heat is more likely to stay productive if you build a culture in which lots of people have the will and the skills to speak to common purpose and to remind others about where they share common ground.

- **Spending a bit more time diagnosing a situation is a leadership behavior.** In tough situations most people look for an easy explanation that blames another group. Enough people practicing the leadership skill of deep diagnosis can disrupt that norm, keeping the heat focused on multiple interpretations rather than a lone scapegoat.

The point is that when everyone leads, lots of people help hold the group in the productive zone; it's not all on one person's shoulders. (More on the productive zone in the next chapter.)

No Heat, No Change

Oil won't boil all by itself. You get nothing if you don't turn on the flame.

Be aware of shying away from heat and getting stuck in work avoidance. It is tempting to assume that anytime things get hot it's "too hot." Discomfort, uncertainty, and conflict (aka heat) are essential ingredients in the recipe for progress on our most important challenges. Inability to deal with conflict productively is one of the reasons our biggest challenges persist, year after year.

We don't want to eliminate conflict; instead we want to engage everyone in keeping conflict productive so that when dealing with it, we make progress on our most important challenges. We need more skills and better processes for bringing conflicting viewpoints to the surface.

As our friend Eric Liu from Citizen University often says, "We don't need fewer arguments in this country. We need better arguments!"

MAKING IT REAL

Dear Ed and Julia,

I am the vice president of a large regional bank with over 1,000 employees. A few years ago the executive team decided to embrace DEI (diversity, equity, and inclusion). Since then, the company has been recognized with numerous community awards for our DEI training, which is a source of pride for many in our company.

But here's the thing: I'm noticing a lot of people are silent during our DEI trainings. They shut down, do the training, and go through the motions. I care deeply about advancing DEI, but I don't want it to just be a check-the-box kind of thing.

And lately there has been one problem employee. He is a manager and has been with the company for many years. He has a lot of credibility and authority. He has been complaining about the DEI training and openly making fun of it. He posts memes about people being overly "woke" on company message boards. I'll probably need to fire him if his behavior doesn't change soon, but I worry that if I do so, it will send a message that our DEI efforts aren't open for examination and critique, which would just lead to more silence and check-the-box mindset from others.

There is so much heat baked into this DEI stuff. How do I navigate all this?

—Amara Awaiting Answers

Dear Amara,

Thank you for championing such an important cause in your company. We share your commitment to DEI. It may be the most important issue of our time.

Yes, it is full of heat, tension, and conflict. We can't avoid those things. Progress requires that you face, talk about, and explore your way through the tough stuff.

Our experience is that the best DEI-related efforts—the ones that actually mobilize others to exercise more inclusive and equitable behaviors—create environments where robust discussion is safe and celebrated. Here's an interpretation to consider:

DEI efforts used to create too little heat: They celebrated our differences but shied away from important subjects like privilege and systemic racism.

Now some DEI efforts—perhaps including ones in your company—might be too hot, creating a fight or flight response from many. Your problem employee might represent the "fight" and your silent employees might represent the "flight."

People can't learn when they are in fight or flight mode. But progress on DEI requires learning! See the dilemma? To get learning, you need vigorous and robust discussion, where people are able and willing to challenge ideas and consider multiple interpretations.

For example, you need people to be able to question whether they contribute to systemic racism without feeling they will be labeled racist.

Great advancements and best practices are emerging in the DEI space, but it's still new territory for many. Advancing DEI is an adaptive challenge. There isn't an exact instruction manual. What works in your company might be differentthan what works in another. Experimentation is key. The presence of healthy conflict, showing up via robust, authentic, and appreciative discussion, tells you the heat is at the right level.

19
In the Productive Zone

We've covered a lot of ground so far in this book. We separated leadership from authority and clarified that the activity of leadership is available to everyone because each of us has at least some small sphere of influence. We've made the case that opportunities to exercise leadership show up in little moments, and these are coming at us constantly, even though most of us haven't learned how to see them yet, let alone seize them. It's hard to transform such a moment into an intervention with lasting impact. We've proposed that we make progress on our toughest challenges when enough people can see these moments, have the courage to seize them, and have the skill to do so successfully.

Martin Luther King Jr.'s "I Have a Dream" speech was an exercise of leadership because it raised the heat on white Americans, effectively helping them focus on the inequality in America. Five years later after King was assassinated and anger raged in most major cities in America, Robert Kennedy lowered the heat in downtown Indianapolis by empathizing with those in mourning and by asking them to channel their energy into love, prayer, and connection rather than bitterness, anger, and hate. Although these are historic and dramatic examples, the need for the same thing—the raising and lowering of heat—exists within our organizations, companies, and communities. And you don't need to be famous, or in a high-authority position, to practice seeing and seizing opportunities to raise or lower the heat.

It's tempting to think of leadership as a magical, ambiguous power. It's not. Simply put, you are exercising leadership when you recognize moments when the heat needs to be raised or lowered to help a group be productive on what matters most.

Most often heat rises and falls around an adaptive challenge without much strategy or purposeful intervention. Just as the temperature outside fluctuates depending on weather patterns, so too does the temperature go up and down in relation to difficult problems facing organizations, companies, and communities.

Much like Goldilocks and the porridge that was not too hot, not too cold, but just right, an optimal level of heat compels people to pay attention to the same challenge long enough for change to occur. Not enough heat and nothing happens. Too much heat and conflict and drama shut down or short circuit opportunities for progress. The goal is to help a group stay at that place in between too hot and too cold. You want the perfect temperature to create useful dissatisfaction with the status quo.

It's so tempting to believe progress can happen without making anyone uncomfortable. It's just not possible with adaptive challenges.

Progress on Adaptive Challenges Is Evolution, Not Revolution

Ron Heifetz and Marty Linsky chose the word *adaptive* because they saw that progress on our toughest problems requires the kind of adaptation we see in nature. Species that are able to adapt to changing environments survive and thrive. The same is true for groups and organizations, communities and countries.

A chimpanzee and a human share 98 percent of their DNA. Just as the evolutionary process changes little DNA of a species, successfully navigating a tough challenge facing your organization doesn't have to mean throwing out all the old ways of doing things. It's about keeping what works and shedding what doesn't. It's evolution not revolution. Small changes over time matter.

The good news is, unlike species that are slowly evolving at the cellular level, we can think ahead about the adaptations we need. For example,

- A 100-year-old family-owned bank in the center of town can recognize it must adapt its traditional model to meet customer expectations or risk losing those customers.

- A college football coach can recognize his team must adapt to the wide-open style of offense most other teams run these days.

- A school district can recognize it must adapt to serve the increasing number of nonnative speakers.

Change Won't Happen Unless You Bring on the Heat

Recognizing the need to adapt is one thing. Mobilizing people to do so is another. The heat has to be high enough for long enough to create change. And remember, no one is unconditionally afraid of change. If the change is all good, we'll take it. We resist change that brings loss.

The bank we just mentioned became a corporate pillar in town using those traditional practices that were modeled, taught, and handed down within one family for generations. The football coach has a playbook and philosophy about practicing that was a perfect match for how the game used to be played. To invest more in bilingual education, the school district will need to invest less in something else.

You need heat to make these kinds of changes. The right level of heat over a sustained period of time encourages people to take risks, clears the way for purposeful adaptation, and creates better ways of achieving your mission or securing your bottom line.

Why is heat needed for change?

- **People don't change until things get uncomfortable.** Most won't move off the status quo unless it's harder living with the current reality than it is to do the work necessary to create a new one.

- **The right amount of heat captures people's attention.** They tune in rather than tune out. Adaptive challenges require lots of people to do something different for progress to be made. Getting and keeping their attention is key.

- **Tough situations create opportunities for learning.**
  Progress on adaptive challenges requires learning about things like your part of the mess, the values in conflict and the potential losses for you and others. When there is no struggle, tension, or frustration, the deep learning that's necessary just doesn't happen. People can learn facts and figures without much conflict or tension, but the type of learning that leads to behavior change only comes with adversity.

In her book *The Art of Gathering*, Priya Parker encourages "good controversy." She encourages healthy group processes where the heat is high enough to be "generative rather than preservationist." Good controversy is our aspiration too. Lasting change can't happen without it.

The Productive Zone of Disequilibrium

Almost every time we teach a group about heat or help a company think about how much discomfort is necessary to generate lasting change, we share a concept called the *productive zone of disequilibrium.*

Getting people over the *threshold of learning* is key. This is the level at which people become uncomfortable enough with the status quo that they get curious about what they need to learn and what habits or behaviors they need to change. Below that threshold people stay busy working on technical stuff and avoiding tough, adaptive work.

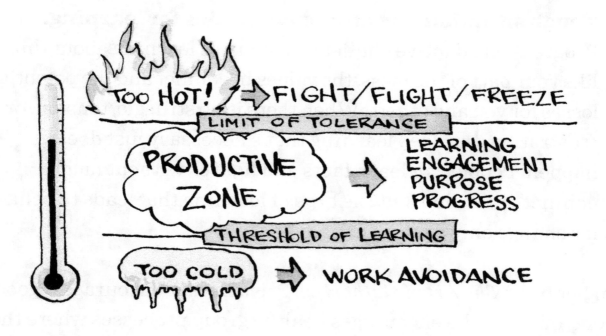

Keeping people under the *limit of tolerance* is key too. An organization can only take so much heat without there being lasting damage to relationships and morale.

Between the threshold of learning and the limit of tolerance is the *productive zone*. You know when you are in it. This is where the adaptive work happens. You are learning, charting new ground, engaging new voices, and every once in a while, you have a sense, perhaps fleeting, that together you are making progress on the challenge at the center of your work. People begin to feel a sense of shared purpose, and you realize that—at least for the moment—you have enough of the right people engaged and doing work. People are taking steps to change their own habits and ways of working, and by doing that, they are helping your system adapt to embrace a new reality. You are in the productive zone when the right people care enough to do something different. At this point, lots of people are involved. Your tough problem has become a collective challenge on its way to a solution.

We Get More Productive When Everyone Leads

Our research and experience suggest progress is all about the actions and leadership from lots of people in a group, organization, or system. A group gets and stays in the productive zone not because one individual (or even one executive team) is exercising leadership, but thanks to the leadership of countless individuals, including some whose interventions to turn up the heat or keep it in the productive zone go unrecognized.

It's like crowd surfing, that crazy activity of people lying on the top of dozens or hundreds of outstretched arms, often in the stands of American college football games or concerts. Because so many hands are involved, it's light work.

When everyone leads, we stay in the productive zone longer, building tolerance so we can wrestle with conflicting viewpoints on important issues and make progress. When everyone leads, the burden of getting in and staying in the productive zone is shared by the many, not the few.

Organizations and communities will be more successful when we empower and equip people at all levels with theskills to challenge and support one another to stay in the productive zone. When the crowd lifts up the work of leadership, many hands make lighter work and tough challenges get seen and solved better and faster.

MAKING IT REAL

Dear Ed and Julia,

I don't think conflict needs to be part of making things better. Let me give you an example from church. We are going through a lot of transition. Key people have left the church after disagreements about how involved we should get with race issues and whether we should have female ministers. And now you are saying we need more conflict to do the adaptive work! But does adaptive work really have to mean tension and conflict? I'm so tired of being at odds with people. Please tell me there is another way!

—Andie Doesn't Want Anyone Angry Anymore

Dear Andie,

We are sorry you've been through such a tough time. Here's the thing: The productive zone, while hard, feels pretty good. It's when you're in the "flow" as some artists and athletes say. It's not the absence of conflict, but good conflict. It's not easy, but it feels worthwhile. It's an experience that leaves you feeling tired, but optimistic.

It sounds to us that the conflict and tension you've been experiencing have not been productive. Maybe things have become too hot?

You might share the productive zone diagram with others in the church and ask where they think you all are. Get others focused on the heat. Encourage them to seize little moments to lead. Together, you will find your way!

Part Five

Everyone Can Lead

Having come this far in a book called *When Everyone Leads*, we hope you are raring to go, eager to exercise more leadership where you live, work, or volunteer. And you may be wondering how to help other people see and seize their moments to lead.

Even after you recognize The Gap, understand the barriers to making progress on tough, adaptive challenges, and acknowledge the need to get the heat in the productive zone, you may be asking, "So where do I start?"

The next four chapters answer that question. Read on to learn how to:

- Ask powerful questions.
- Make multiple interpretations.
- Act experimentally.
- Make leadership less risky for others.

20

Everyone Can Ask Powerful Questions

It's tempting to think leadership is a superhero saving the day, a president galvanizing a nation, a captain rallying a team to victory.

That "leader as savior" mythology focuses our attention on whoever is in charge—hoping and expecting them to solve the problem, right the ship, make things better. If we are the ones in charge, the "leader as savior" mindset diverts us from engaging others in problem-solving and drives us towardquick fixes without deep diagnosis of the situation.

Diagnosis is fueled by questions. Good questions generate better interpretations and lead to better interventions. Good questions sometimes raise the heat and sometimes work wonders to lower the heat and keep groups in the productive zone.

Albert Einstein famously said, "If I had an hour to solve a problem and my life depended on it, I would use the first 55 minutes determining the proper questions to ask."

Asking questions is a leadership skill that is available to anyone. It's one of the simplest (though not always easy) ways for people without authority to exercise leadership. Take these examples:

- A young professional, after participating in a three-hour meeting covering dozens of topics, meets with their manager and asks, "Of all the topics we just discussed, what is most critical for our success over the next month? I'm confused about how all this fits together." That question won't change the world, but it might help the manager realize people are wondering where to focus.

- A small business has been losing customers. At a staff meeting an employee asks, "What story might our customers be telling about us and how is it different from the one we tell ourselves?" That question could elicit some pretty important introspection for the struggling business.

- A math teacher notices no evidence of concern among school staff, despite major challenges such as an increasing percentage of students from impoverished families. At the beginning of a staff meeting the teacher asks, "What would be a good outcome for this meeting and how does it connect to our biggest challenges?" That question might nudge the group to be more purposeful.

- Two friends who work at the same organization are out to lunch. One shares how frustrated she is with her boss. The other empathizes, but instead of fanning the flames of discontent, asks, "What is your team's most important challenge right now?" and "Where do you suppose your boss feels stuck?" These questions could shift the friend's attitude from frustration to curiosity, helping her put the challenge (not the person) at the center of her work.

What Makes a Powerful Question?

Powerful questions invite people to explore multiple perspectives. Questions that illuminate adaptive challenges are not the same as those a lawyer would use to interrogate a witness. These questions aren't trying to box someone in or prove a point. Instead they are open-ended, provoke reflection, and can seldom be answered with one word. They lead to curiosity and discovery. Think back to how we started this book by encouraging you to pose questions like these: "What are your greatest aspirations?" and "What concerns you the most?"

When you are trying to make progress on a leadership challenge, powerful questions can help you:

- Create consensus about the leadership challenge.
- Identify who is most affected by the problem (and thus who needs to be engaged to solve it).
- Explore perspectives.
- Understand root causes.
- Clarify collective purpose.
- Open minds to alternative approaches.
- Help others see moments to exercise leadership.
- Raise the heat in large groups, team meetings, and one-on-one conversations.
- Expose unspoken barriers, shared values, or big aspirations.

Sequencing Powerful Questions

When exercising leadership on a daunting challenge, there is skill in knowing what kind of questions to ask, and when. In general, you want questions that propel more curiosity and discovery early in conversations or projects. Later you'll want questions that drive to action, experimentation, and commitment.

In the beginning of a conversation or project, ask questions like these:

1. What would be a good outcome for this conversation (meeting, process, etc.)?
2. What's important to you about this?
3. What would someone with a very different set of beliefs have to say about this?
4. What's our intention here?
5. What is our deeper purpose?
6. What is worth our best effort?

In the middle of a conversation or project, ask questions like these:

1. What do we know so far and what do we still need to learn?
2. What assumptions do we need to test or challenge?
3. What's taking shape?
4. What are we hearing underneath the variety of opinions being expressed?
5. What new connections are we making?
6. What's missing?

7. What are we not seeing?

8. If there was one thing that hasn't been said yet, what would it be?

In the end of a conversation or project, ask questions like these:

1. How will we experiment?

2. What's possible here and how committed are we?

3. What will progress look like?

4. How can we support each other in taking next steps?

5. What unique contribution can we each make?

6. As we move forward, what challenges might come our way?

7. How will we meet those challenges?

8. What will it mean to stick to purpose?

It's Not Always Easy to Ask a Powerful Question

Asking powerful questions is a leadership move that is available to any of us, no matter our position in an organization or community. But that doesn't mean it's always easy. Things (including ourselves) can get in the way. As you start asking powerful questions, remember:

- **You must genuinely want to help others engage in difficult work.** If you are most concerned about getting information for yourself, then your questions will be self-serving. You'll ask things like "When does the meeting start?" "Am I supposed to be there?" and "What do we need to do before we get there?" You might really need to know the answers to those questions, but they are about you, not about others. Leadership is about mobilizing others. Your questions need to serve them.

They need to inspire others to think or engage differently around a challenge.

- **Don't overinflate the risk of interjecting a question.** Leadership is always risky, but asking a powerful question is one of the least risky actions you can take. Questions suggest a direction for the discussion and invite people into the productive zone. It might be out of the group norm for someone like you to ask powerful questions, but the risk is likely minimal, especially if you pick the right type of question for the moment. Inflating the risk involved is one of the ways we let ourselves off the hook.

- **Resist "gotcha" questions.** Politicians resort too often to gotcha questions. Silly example: "Would you rather vote for my opponent who wants to raise your taxes, take away your puppy and make the sale of chocolate illegal, or for me?" Gotcha questions are designed not to help a group, but to embarrass someone or box someone into a corner. When dealing with heated issues it can be natural to have a strong point of view. Sharing that point of view can be fine. Debating is fine too. But those who exercise leadership find ways to manage themselves, to keep their emotions in check, and to build relationships across divides. Curious, open, and engaging questions help you manage your own emotions and provide a pathway for others to manage theirs. Gotcha questions do the opposite.

- **Avoid "suquestions."** That's when your question is really a suggestion. If you have a suggestion, make it. But don't pretend it's a question. "Have you ever thought about . . .?" and "What would you think of the idea of . . .?" are suggestions disguised as questions. Powerful questions come from a place of curiosity. They are motivated by a desire to help an individual or group access their own creativity and find their way forward.

- **Free yourself from the need to ask the perfect question.** A friend of ours was in the midst of a tense and too hot discussion when, not knowing what to do, he glanced at our list of "good in the middle questions." He raised his voice and lobbed out the first question that caught his eye: "What assumptions do we need to test or challenge?" People took a collective deep breath. The ensuing discussion lowered the heat right before his eyes. There is no perfect question. Almost any open-ended question by our friend in that meeting would have had the same heat-lowering effect.

- **Use silence.** When you pose an open-ended question, take care that you don't rush in to answer it yourself. Give the other person time to reflect. Allow space for a powerful question to land in the heart or gut so it can generate energy for adaptive work.

It's interesting, isn't it, how few good questions get asked in organizations. Most of us go days without hearing a genuinely curious question. Keeping a group in the productive zone is everyone's work. The heat stays hot enough when enough people in a system or organization are prepared to ask questions that matter. Leadership is about seeing and seizing moments. The simplest way to do that can be to notice what question would help propel the group forward right now.

Having lots of people in your organization skilled in asking powerful questions is like deploying an army of executive coaches. Everyone will be asking powerful questions that help peers, direct reports, and even supervisors see and seize more moments to lead. Every time someone asks a good question, they do their part to build a culture where everyone leads.

MAKING IT REAL

Dear Ed and Julia,

I'm a volunteer with a food pantry. The founders run everything with the help of just a few volunteers like me. The pantry has done good work to uplift and protect community members during difficult times. But it's never done much to engage people beyond those founders and their friends. The pantry could have more impact if we had more community support. The answer is partnerships and I've worked to connect the pantry to other organizations focused on ending food insecurity. No one has done anything with my ideas and lately I've been grappling with whether it is even my place to share them. Thoughts?

—Volunteer Vincente

Dear Vincente,

Try shifting your approach from promoter-of-ideas to asker-of-questions. Get super-curious about what each of the founders wants for the people you serve. Ask questions that invite them to articulate their dreams for how the pantry could have more impact. Don't wait for meetings or formal opportunities. Ask questions during volunteer shifts and when you see someone around town.

Release yourself from the pressure of making the founders see that partnerships are the way forward. Frame questions that help them reconnect to why they started the pantry in the first place. Ask their opinion about the biggest barriers to eliminating food insecurity in your community. Maybe your questions will lead them to that idea or maybe you'll inspire a different, but better, approach.

21
Everyone Can Make Multiple Interpretations

How we think about a problem determines how we try to solve it. Change or evolve our thinking and we might discover ways for more progress. Imagine these situations:

- A seventh-grader is routinely late for school. His single mom, exhausted from juggling two jobs and raising three kids, thinks he doesn't wake up early enough. She buys him an alarm clock and scolds him for not waking up earlier. But what if he is getting bullied in the hallway before school starts? The alarm clock and scolding won't help that situation.

- A small business owner keeps losing employees and thinks it's because the economy is struggling. Knowing he can't control the broader economy, he just keeps complaining and looking for new employees. But what if the workplace culture is toxic or uninspiring? An economic turnaround won't fix that.

- A political party wins big in one election only to lose disastrously in the next. The party chair is sure it's because the opposition party used a cultural wedge issue to stir up voters. The chair releases talking points for party members: The wedge issue isn't really an issue; it's all make-believe. But what if the root cause of the big defeat is the party losing touch with everyday voters? Those talking points won't help.

Every leadership effort starts with collecting information. The mom heard from the school that her kid is always late. The business owner saw that employees were quitting. The party chair couldn't help but notice the disastrous election results.

And in most cases, with just a few observations, we make an interpretation about what's going on. The mom decides the boy is oversleeping. The business owner decides it's the economy's fault. The chair decides he knows what the issue is.

Usually our quick interpretation justifies a relatively easy response, lacking any deep diagnosis. The mom scolds and buys an alarm clock. The business owner complains and hires new employees. The party chair sends out talking points and then returns to business as usual.

So our actions can be traced back to our interpretations and those can be traced back to our observations. We constantly and often unconsciously go through these steps.

When the challenge is a complex one, we need leadership that helps others go through these steps many times.

Push Beyond Your First Idea

A prerequisite for progress is to think about the problem differently. More observations generate more interpretations and more possible actions. Let's revisit our three examples one more time:

- What if that mom also observes that, in fact, they always arrive at the school 10 minutes before classes start, but her son fidgets nervously in the car until a certain group of kids walks into the building? She might start to wonder if being late is a way to avoid something uncomfortable at school in the morning.

- What if that business owner also observes unkind gossip and treatment of new employees by the tenured staff? He might start to wonder if in addition to hiring new staff he might need to get rid of some of the old ones.

- What if the party chair observes that a host of things the party is pushing are proving unpopular and that the wedge issue alone might not explain the negative turn? Those talking points about the "nonissue wedge issue" might be accompanied by other actions to figure out what's going on.

We encourage people to push past their first interpretations to generate others that point toward more-difficult-to-execute action steps. If you find yourself resisting an interpretation because addressing it would involve loss and discomfort, you're probably on to something. Tougher interpretations are the ones most likely to lead to lasting progress on our most difficult problems.

When you engage a group to consider multiple tough interpretations, you are inviting them to consider conflicting versions of the truth—not so they can act on each one but so they can choose which interpretations are worth exploring further.

Julia was coaching a group of people from different departments at a big university. The biggest challenge facing the director of the information technology center was completing a university-wide software update that had dragged on (he was ashamed to say) for years. One of the many issues embedded in the bigger challenge was that a handful of professors were refusing to abandon their ancient word processing software and join everyone else in the 21st century. As he listened to peers diagnose his challenge, the director suddenly saw that he'd been hanging on to one unhelpful interpretation: that the professors' behavior was a personal attack on him—that they didn't like him or trust his team and were taking this opportunity to show it. Once the IT director considered other interpretations (that, for instance, the professors might value their current mastery over the ancient technology more than they appreciate the need for the update), he understood that by taking their pushback personally, he was part of the mess. Having implicated himself, a range of new options for action appeared.

When the Challenge Is Adaptive, We Need Everyone Offering Tough Interpretations

One interpretation from one person won't work when the challenge is adaptive. To solve our toughest problems, we need diverse points of view and multiple interpretations. It is an exercise of leadership to encourage others to bring more data and imagine more explanations for what's happening.

During the 1960s President Johnson was adamant that the best way to help the disadvantaged and marginalized in the United States would be a "war on poverty." The issue was close to his heart and he passionately believed in the cause. The movie *Selma* wonderfully depicts a scene in the White House where Martin Luther King Jr. disrupts President Johnson's thinking. Johnson politely rebuffs King's request for civil rights legislation and instead tells him the war on poverty is the best way to help marginalized people in America. King offers a tougher interpretation: until Black Americans have full access to the ballot box, antipoverty measures won't help. It's a profound moment in their relationship and in the civil rights movement of the 1960s. Eventually, Johnson agrees and the two successfully push the civil rights legislation into law.

Why Is It Hard to Offer Multiple, Tough Interpretations?

Few of us have the confidence, courage, and discipline of Martin Luther King Jr. Four things get in the way of making more and tougher interpretations:

1. A lack of agency. We may not think it's our job to question the way our organization, department, or company is thinking about a problem, especially if we have little authority in the system. Even if we have a clear purpose and a good chance of making things better, we stay quiet rather than muster the courage to speak up.

2. It's risky. Suggesting to others that there is more to consider is suggesting that they haven't thought about the situation clearly. Ideally they will welcome the input. But they could bristle at what feels like a correction.

3. It requires us to collect a lot more data. We have to slow down and think more about what's going on in the situation. We have to look up from the day to day and take a good look around. We have to talk to other people and try to see things through their eyes.

4. We have to be willing to be wrong. The point of making multiple interpretations isn't to find the right or the perfect explanation. The point is to make interpretations that are worth considering, that reveal complexities and potential opportunities for change. We have to be willing to offer and explore half-baked ideas.

What Becomes Possible When More People Offer Multiple, Tough Interpretations?

When more people offer tough interpretations, groups stay in the productive zone longer. It's a way to ward off work avoidance and to keep people focused on a big challenge.

A culture that values tough interpretations reduces groupthink. People have permission to suggest alternative ways of seeing. They feel compelled to help one another see the full picture. When people regularly provoke one another to come up with different explanations for a problem their team is less likely to line up blindly behind the wrong way forward.

MAKING IT REAL

Dear Ed and Julia,

I work in local government and am hosting an upcoming meeting to discuss the challenge of creating a community free of discrimination, racism, and injustice. The impetus for the meeting was the publication of a comprehensive (and provocative!) report detailing dozens of community issues (homelessness, crime, education, affluence, health, etc.) broken down by race.

Historically, our city government tends to shy away from discussions like this, with department heads quickly pointing out that we always treat everyone the same in the city. But this new data tells a different story.

The meeting is only 90 minutes. A number of community stakeholders along with department heads from across city government will attend. I know we can't solve all issues of discrimination and racism in 90 minutes, but I want this to be productive. Any advice?

—Isabel Is Inciting Interpretations

Dear Isabel,

It sounds like you have a great opportunity to help the group generate multiple interpretations about a critical subject. Think of the report as a big set of observations about your community. Spend the bulk of the meeting asking the group to offer multiple interpretations of the data in the report.

Let people know that you aren't looking for group consensus. You are after a deep diagnosis; you're trying to help everyone more thoroughly make sense of the data from different perspectives. Push people to be open to multiple interpretations. Use language such as "One interpretation is . . . Another interpretation is . . . And yet another interpretation is. . . ."

We'd encourage you to go ahead and set up a second meeting. Make it clear that this one is for deep diagnosis (multiple interpretations) and the second will be to come up with initial actions (we call them experiments) based on those interpretations.

Thank you for taking on this important conversation!

22
Everyone Can Act Experimentally

Julia was a professional actor. Ed dabbled in theater as a young adult. Improv games and drills were a staple of Julia's professional training. Ed performed improv comedy with a group of friends once a week during one college summer. While neither of us were accomplished enough to make it on *Whose Line Is It Anyway?*, we took good lessons about leadership from our improv days.

You learn a lot about yourself when you stand in front of an audience, without a script, and have no idea what to say or do next. All eyes are on you and the audience is expecting you to make them laugh. It is frightening and liberating at the same time. You learn to stay present, listen deeply, and then just try something. It might work, meaning it might be funny. Even if it's not funny, it might create something that allows someone else on stage to do something funny. Or whatever you do could completely fail, falling flat with a big, giant thud of silence all around you. But even then, the failure is short-lived. Someone tries something else, the audience laughs, and the game goes on.

You just need to keep trying things, working with your partners, and experimenting your way to raucous laughter.

Improvisational comedy is an experimental art. Leadership is an experimental art, too. As with improv, you can't be sure what will work. What got people to laugh last night might not work tonight. What worked to mobilize people around that challenge last month might not work with the challenge you face this month.

Successful improv comedy requires a steady stream of set-ups from partners, jokes that land, good use of silence, and surprising moments. We might say that a series of experiments gets people into the productive "humor" zone. The actors know they need to hold people in that zone, but what works will be different night to night, moment to moment. Getting and keeping people in the zone requires every actor to experiment. Sometimes audience members experiment too, offering topics and suggestions for scenes, occasionally even joining actors on stage.

Progress on adaptive challenges requires a steady stream of people seeing their moment to jump on stage and move the group forward. With leadership, like improv, seizing your moment is always an experiment. With improv, you don't know if a joke will work until you try it. With leadership, you don't know if your action will have an impact until you try it.

Cultivate a Culture of Experimentation

We use the word *experiment* a lot in our work. We use it to mean an action, activity, project, or initiative undertaken in hopes of making progress on a tough challenge. The word makes sense because no one knows exactly how to solve an adaptive challenge. Therefore everything is a bit of an experiment.

Adaptive work requires multiple, successive experiments. A single experiment is rarely, if ever, sufficient to solve (or make lasting progress on) an adaptive challenge. That's why we talk about acting experimentally and cultivating an experimental mindset. In a culture in which everyone leads, people at all levels embrace an experimental mindset.

Acting experimentally is especially useful for three reasons:

1. Experiments contribute to deep diagnosis of a challenge.
When exercising leadership, you experiment not to solve the presenting problem, but to learn more about the problem, how people feel about it, what's holding back progress, and so on. All that learning, which we call *deep diagnosis*, eventually leads to powerful interventions to spur progress on the issue. It's like a scientist early in her work battling a new virus. She doesn't yet know much about the virus, what it is, or how it works. At first, her experiments focus simply on learning more. She focuses later experiments on finding solutions.

2. Experiments help define possible solutions. Experiments are also necessary to test possible solutions. When the challenge is adaptive, we don't know exactly what will work. Running experiments—trying lots of things at once—is a productive and efficient way of discovering what might work. When the pandemic took hold in March 2020, KLC launched an array of experiments within a few days, trying out new ways of delivering value to our partners and clients. The diversity of those experiments helped us learn what worked, what didn't, and what deserved more of our attention.

3. Experiments get and keep a group in the productive zone. Some experiments are less about the content of your problem and more about the way your group tries to solve the problem. A company might experiment with asking a task force to go away for a week to work on a problem. A team might experiment with a new way of conducting its meetings, hoping to generate more robust discussion rather than mundane reports. An extrovert might experiment by not speaking up first, testing whether that creates space for others to engage.

The most complex and entrenched challenges require people to act experimentally over generations. For instance, in the seven decades leading up to the passage of the 19th Amendment to the U.S. Constitution, supporters of women's right to vote held conventions, drafted resolutions, and passed laws at the state level. Each of these moves was an experiment designed to make progress on the big, daunting adaptive challenge. Activist women marched. They were jeered at and beaten but their action moved the challenge forward. They voted illegally and allowed themselves to be arrested, and their experiments drew attention to the cause. Some people experimented in the heat of public scrutiny, while countless others tried everything to change neighbors' minds and get elected representatives to vote their way. Sometimes suffragists stuck together and other times their experiments diverged.

Even with the ratification of the 19th Amendment on August 26, 1920, the need to experiment continued. Indigenous American women didn't gain the right to vote until the 1950s and many Black women couldn't participate in elections until the Voting Rights Act of 1965. Progress on our toughest challenges takes lifetimes and lasting change means multitudes acting experimentally, one intervention, a lot of learning, and a little bit of progress at a time.

When Everyone Leads, We All Act Experimentally

Just like an improv company needs all its actors to try lots of jokes, progress on adaptive challenges requires lots of people to do their part, run experiments to keep the heat at a healthy simmer, and move the group forward to success.

It's tricky, though. It runs against the quick-fix mentality. It's also hard to accept that not everything we try will work. When you embrace an experimental mindset, you embrace failure. Many of your leadership experiments won't work! That's why we call them experiments.

Acting experimentally is risky. But when enough people in an organization, company, or community embrace an experimental mindset, we reach a tipping point. Experiments become a hallmark of our culture. Smart risks and the occasional failure become the norm. People back up one another's experiments and help one another learn.

You don't have to be the person in charge to embrace an experimental mindset. You just have to show up believing that you have all the authority you need to see a moment where leadership could happen, do something, review how it worked, and go from there. Bring your curious, experimental mindset to every meeting that could be more productive, every group that needs an energy boost, and every relationship with the potential for greater meaning. That's how you create a culture where everyone leads.

MAKING IT REAL

> **Dear Ed and Julia,**
>
> **I'm playing with this new model of leadership. I want to experiment. But I need more ideas. Help!**
>
> **—Lettie the Leadership Junky**

Dear Lettie,

Thank you for writing. Our first question is: What is driving your desire to experiment? What is the change you want to make in the world? Remember leadership always starts with an aspiration to make progress on a tough challenge. Once you've identified the challenge, a simple but valuable experiment could be talking to other people about it. Whose perspective are you interested in? Who might see the challenge differently than you do? Who would need to play a role in your change effort? Who might feel reluctant to get involved (and why)?

Another category of experiments could be related to making yourself heard: Who needs to hear your perspective on the problem? Who needs to know how much you care? Who might respond to your invitation to contribute ideas and work for change?

Experiments don't have to be bombastic but they always involve other people. And they may require you to step outside your comfort zone. You'll find a whole boatload (or shall we say, a whole book-load) of ideas for experiments in KLC's book, *Your Leadership Edge: Strategies and Tools for When Everyone Leads.*

23
Make Leadership Less Risky for Others

When someone successfully seizes a moment to exercise leadership what they are really doing is quite disruptive. In time their efforts may be remembered for turning the tide of a whole project and setting a group up for success. But in the moment many of those around them will be likely to resist the disruption. People will push back on hard questions, perceiving them as attacks on their competence. They will reject the person who dared to question the standard approach, or sideline them as punishment for elevating errors. Here are a few examples:

- A frustrated project team has spent half of its regular meeting complaining about how so-and-so from another team is screwing things up for the company. As the clock ticks away on their time together a teammate who has been quiet for most of the meeting interjects a quick line: "Well we've spent half our meeting complaining about others. How about we spend the next half talking about our part of the mess?" That little intervention disrupts conversation and might even put colleagues on the defensive.

"Take as much time as you need."

- A board of directors of a nonprofit has grown accustomed to monthly one-hour meetings. It's enough time to approve the minutes and financials and go over some key metrics, but at least one person recognizes that it is never enough time to dig into the big questions facing the organization. That board member suggests a day-long strategy session to dig into the really important stuff, immediately spawning headaches and creating conflicts for other board members. Some staff members, too, prefer the board be kept at a distance. For this organization, this suggestion has been disruptive.

- A high school basketball team isn't playing up to its potential through the first half of the season. At a players' meeting called by the captain, an underclassman points out that most of the team only does the bare minimum of practice. She notes that few of the players arrive earlyor stay late to work on the individual skills so critical for basketball success. That comment is disruptive, calling into question the individual commitment of the players.

These examples all involve someone seeing and seizing a moment to intervene in hopes of helping their group move forward. The teammate, board member, and underclassman are all taking a bit of risk. They are interrupting the flow and changing the tenor of conversation. They are going against the norm. They are opening themselves up to being ignored, ridiculed, or sidelined by the group. Seizing even small moments to exercise leadership is risky.

When someone questions a norm or names a potentially unproductive pattern, it raises the heat (at least for a moment) and opens the door for their group to learn and evolve. If they are part of a culture in which everyone leads, people will likely respond favorably.

But if, like most companies, organizations, or communities, yours has not yet reached leadership heaven, where everyone is always ready to jump immediately into the productive zone, the person in your system who does the disrupting will need some help to make their intervention stick.

Use Your Influence or Authority to Protect People Who Seize Moments to Lead

In the frustrated project team example, for instance, support for the provocateur could come from the project lead saying, "Good point! There has to be some part of this mess that's ours. Let's get to work on us."

The board chair in our second example could be the first to agree to the day-long strategy session, underlining the impact it could have on the organization's ability to meet its mission. The chair could help bring others along by acknowledging that this will be something new for everyone and may take some personal sacrifices to get scheduled.

The team captain could thank the underclassman for being brave enough to name the need to improve skills and teamwork. The captain could pledge to show up early for practice the next day and invite others to join.

Limit Risk and Keep the Group in the Productive Zone

Leveraging your influence or authority to make leadership less risky for others raises and lowers the heat at the same time. It raises the heat on those who would rather ignore a problem, and at the same time, it steals fuel from any effort to discredit or disempower the disruptor.

Using your influence or authority to support and celebrate disruptions lowers the heat in situations in which people might otherwise respond to a provocative statement with disdain, distress, or anger, or by disassociating themselves from the person who delivered it.

The support of someone in authority is often the only thing that can keep the disruptor from losing status or being completely ostracized by the group. In cases where a team member sees a moment but seizes it clumsily, a nod from authority shows that it's not the end of the world if your leadership intervention didn't land quite the way you'd intended it. If the boss models curiosity and appreciation, other people have a chance to recalibrate their emotions enough to seek value in what the disruptor is offering.

Here are two more examples of how a person in authority can step in to lower the heat, help people listen curiously, and partner with a disruptor to make progress on an important challenge:

- A young professional brings up a difficult topic in an all-staff meeting. He does it in a clunky way that leaves people feeling confused and attacked. Anyone on the staff with more positional authority could realize what the young person is trying to accomplish and work with him, in front of everyone, to help make the intention clearer. The more senior person could say, "I think I see where you are going with this, Todd. What you are getting at is that we are, through no ill will on anyone's part, ignoring a key partner because we are afraid of what we will hear from them if we start asking questions. Do I have that right?" In this example the person in authority strengthens Todd's leadership attempt while lowering the heat to a potentially productive level by partnering with him to dispel any confusion about intent.

- A social worker in a nonprofit advocating for sentencing reform invites opponents to a meeting to see if common ground can be found. They get the warring factions to show up but haven't thought through how to structure the discussion so it will be productive. The meeting quickly devolves into a boisterous argument. Other staff members are angry about the setback. Although it would be easy for the person in the top job to join those heaping blame on the social worker, instead the executive director applauds the effort and shoulders the blame herself for not providing time and space to think through the engagement. By shielding the social worker from negative consequences, the executive director reduces the heat in the system and gets everyone refocused on the important challenge of finding an approach to sentencing reform that most people can live with. The executive director's move also makes it clear that people in her organization who take risks on behalf of purpose will not be punished. Instead they will be encouraged to get out there and try again.

When people who rock the boat are protected and celebrated, it makes it more likely that others will step up and intervene too.

Live Like Thomas

We were blessed with a curious and sometimes maddeningly frustrating colleague named Thomas Stanley. He started at KLC as a 22-year-old college graduate with zero professional experience. He died tragically in 2019 after 11 wonderful years as a key contributor to KLC. We talk about him often inside KLC, and what consistently emerges is how well Thomas modeled the KLC leadership idea of *intervene skillfully,* and how he showed us all how worthwhile it is to take risks, to be provocative, and to insist that others do something different. Thomas was always intervening, raising the heat, acting experimentally, and making very purposeful choices to move KLC forward. Some of his leadership moments were wildly successful, helping us take great leaps forward. His other interventions were hit or miss. Some would move things forward a bit, others would fail to generate progress or momentum.

Thomas and Ed had a unique partnership. As CEO Ed recognized the creative, galvanizing spirit of Thomas and wanted it unleashed to help move KLC forward. But he also recognized that some of Thomas's efforts fell flat. Other schemes he had would have frustrated the heck out of people if they were executed as Thomas first conceived of doing them. Ed worked hard to reduce the risks involved for Thomas. He rewarded him when his ideas struck gold and coached him privately when he missed the mark. Ed made leading less risky for Thomas and Thomas responded by seeing and seizing the moments that could use his leadership. For instance, when some of us were satisfied with reaching 1,000 participants a year, Thomas was not. He imagined ways to push well beyond that and now we work with more than 7,000 annually.

Thomas took risks all the time; he made more noticeable mistakes than the rest of us, and yet people saw him get promoted and celebrated. He helped convey that at KLC—in a culture where everyone leads—the expectation is that you will intervene and rock the boat when needed, and that being disruptive is rewarded, not punished. Thomas forever changed KLC and remains one of the best exemplars of an individual who put our ideas of leadership into practice.

Use Your Authority to Make Leadership Less Risky for Others

Great things happen when everyone leads. But just wishing it for yourself, your colleagues, and your neighbors and partners doesn't make it so. Those in authority can do these three things to make exercising leadership less risky for others.

- **Don't just preach, teach!** Invest time or money in building team members' capacity to see and seize moments that need leadership. Create formal and informal ways to help your people learn the skills associated with leading on adaptive challenges. Start by getting everyone a copy of *Your Leadership Edge*. It goes into great detail about what the exercise of leadership in key moments looks like.

- **Notice and celebrate leadership efforts by your team.** Notice when your people try to exercise leadership. Then, whether they succeed or not, celebrate them for seeing a moment for leadership. Encourage them to keep trying to seize those moments. With leadership, failure is always a possibility. Without affirmation from authority, people will become less willing to take the risk. Julia regularly convenes meetings of KLC's world-class team of teachers and coaches and (because this is a highly skilled and ready-to-be-provocative group) she prepares herself mentally for the moment in every meeting when someone will question the way we've always done things. On a good day, her first move is to thank and celebrate the disruptor, and her second move (especially if a critique reflects directly on her decisions) is to coach herself against moving on too quickly from an uncomfortable moment. Her twin goals are to celebrate the disruptor and to partner with that person to generate some productive heat.

- **Normalize talking about leadership as an activity and one that's risky.** A person in authority can make leadership less risky by talking about it incessantly. When people in authority speak often about the idea that leadership is an activity and that it requires taking a few risks, the culture starts to shift. When those at the top profess often that they value leadership and risk, it creates a new mindset. ("The boss wants us to be disruptive, so we'd better be on the lookout for our moments!") Say it often enough, and then watch as more and more people start seeing and seizing their moments to lead.

MAKING IT REAL

> **Dear Ed and Julia,**
>
> Okay, Ed and Julia, all this disruption is starting to seem dangerous. I'm the founder and managing partner of an architecture firm. We'd never get things done if all 100+ employees were constantly interrupting with questions and "leadership interventions," taking us down bunny trails. Where's the balance here? Can I run a business and at the same time cultivate a culture where everyone leads?
>
> **—Alan the Architect**

Alan,

Keep in mind they aren't leading if they are just propelling people down bunny trails. If they are exercising leadership, they should be finding connecting interests and coalescing people around what matters most.

We encourage you to build their capacity to understand what leadership could look like for each of them and support them as they experiment. You'll know you trained them well if their leadership interventions lead to more progress on the most pressing challenges facing the company instead of bunny trails.

One last thought: Our research shows creating a culture of leadership will make it easier for you, the senior authority, to run your business. The more they feel skilled and empowered to lead, the more vested your people will become in the company mission.

24

When Everyone Leads: A Call to Action

The ideas in this book run counter to norms about leadership.

- Leadership is an activity, not a position.

- Leadership is mobilizing others to make progress on our most important challenges.

- Leadership is iterative, risky and experimental.

- And ultimately, it's about progress. No progress? Then you aren't exercising leadership.

- Leadership comes in moments.

- These moments are hard to see, easy to ignore, and require courage and skill to seize them effectively.

- Leadership is always about change.

- Change starts with you.

- No one is afraid of change. They are afraid of loss.

- Leadership is engaging others, weaving connections between people who think differently and value different things.

- Leadership is helping people accept loss. That's why leadership is risky.

- No one exercises leadership without a clear and compelling purpose.

- That's why leadership is worth the risk.

Leadership Is Countercultural

The leadership described in this book is a match for our turbulent times. It is hopeful, forward-looking, and an antidote to hatred and polarization. It could be the only true way forward. The leadership you've read about here places the challenge at the center. It places the common good at the center. And when we place the common good at the center, we realize that although we each have tremendous power to make a difference, our individual power, expertise, and ability will never be enough.

Even the boss of the company or the queen of the country can't make the toughest challenges go away. They can't dictate or manage or authorize or supervise the way to the future they desire. None of us can do it by ourselves.

And that leads to our most countercultural idea:

- It's when everyone leads that our toughest, most important challenges get seen and solved.

A Culture Where Everyone Leads

There may have been times in history (maybe you can remember a time in your company or your country) when just one or two people spurred major progress on a given issue. But today's dynamics are different. The rate of change is too fast. The perspectives on problems are too diverse. Today, progress requires lots of people with the ability to adapt and the skill to mobilize others.

Of course, the exercise of leadership looks different for the CEO versus the line manager versus the front-line employee. But when it comes to our toughest challenges, we each have a piece of the puzzle.

As we build a culture where everyone leads:

- We spend more time in diagnosis.

- We inspire one another by asking, "What are our big aspirations?"

- We slow down and look at The Gap. We identify our toughest challenges.

- We ask more questions and push ourselves to identify multiple, tough interpretations.

- We patiently start where we have influence and humbly identify our piece of the mess.

- We get curious about people who oppose us. We wonder who they care about most, what they value, how they see the situation.

- We experiment all the time. We learn.

- We make more progress.

- And sometimes, as we work across factions, we surprise ourselves by discovering lasting solutions we all can celebrate.

We might even get happier. KLC's research shows those who understand that leadership is an activity are more likely to collaborate and more hopeful about the future. As we contribute to a culture in which everyone leads, we feel more committed to our organizations and more satisfied with our jobs.

How Tough Challenges Get Seen and Solved

We won't solve our toughest challenges by doing more of what we've always done. Don't take this book as a call to get busier or be more determined.

Instead, shift your attention. The world needs more people stepping up to exercise leadership. See what happens if you engage with others differently. Put the challenge at the center and see who you can get to consider it, to offer their view of it, to wonder how they could experiment and contribute to positive change.

Start within your sphere of influence. As you grow your influence, don't be afraid of people with very different viewpoints. Approach them with curiosity. Invite them in. Assume their leadership is as necessary as your own. Let them help you see the challenge more fully. Work with them.

Together is the only way to propel progress on what matters most to ourselves, our organizations, our communities, and our world.

How do tough problems get solved?

People everywhere see and seize their moments to lead.

References

Banwart, Mary, Elnaz Parviz, and Tim Steffensmeier. *Leadership Development and Employee Engagement in Nonprofit Organizations*. Wichita, KS: KLC Press, 2020. https://kansasleadershipcenter.org/third-floor-research/third-floor-research-report-non-profits

Covey, Stephen R. *The 7 Habits of Highly Effective People: Restoring the Character Ethic*. [Rev. ed.]. New York: Free Press, 2004.

DuVernay, Ava, director. *Selma*. Screenplay by Paul Webb. Plan B Entertainment and Cloud Eight Films, 2014.

Ekwerike, Onyedika, Tim Steffensmeier, and Tamas Kowalik. *Weathering the Storm: Leadership Lessons from the 2008 Financial Crisis*. Wichita, KS: KLC Press, 2020. https://kansasleadershipcenter.org/third-floor-research/third-floorresearch-weathering-the-storm

Heifetz, Ronald A. *Leadership without Easy Answers*. Cambridge, MA: Belknap Press of Harvard University Press, 1994.

Heifetz, Ronald A., and Marty Linsky. *Leadership on the Line: Staying Alive through the Dangers of Change*. Boston, MA: Harvard Business Review Press, *2017*.

Heifetz, Ronald A., Marty Linsky, and Alexander Grashow. *The Practice of Adaptive Leadership: Tools and Tactics for Changing Your Organization and the World*. Boston, MA: Harvard Business Press, 2009.

Kahneman, Daniel. *Thinking, Fast and Slow*. New York: Farrar, Straus and Giroux, 2011.

Kahneman, Daniel, Olivier Sibony and Cass R. Sunstein. *Noise: A Flaw in Human Judgment*. New York: Little, Brown Spark, 2021.

Kegan, Robert, and Lisa Laskow Lahey. *Immunity to Change*. Boston, MA: Harvard Business Review Press, 2009.

Kelley, Tom and David Kelley. *Creative Confidence: Unleashing the creative potential within us all*. New York: Crown Business, 2013.

O'Malley, Ed and Amanda Cebula. *Your Leadership Edge: Strategies and Tools for When Everyone Leads*. Austin, TX: Bard Press, 2022.

Parker, Priya. *The Art of Gathering: How We Meet and Why it Matters*. New York: Riverhead Books, 2018.

Steffensmeier, Tim, Tamas Kowalik, Tim O'Brien. *Leadership Development for Global Organizations in the High-tech Industry*. Wichita, KS: KLC Press, 2020. https://kansasleadershipcenter. org/third-floor-research/ third-floor-researchreport-high-tech-industry

Vogt, Eric, Juanita Brown, and David Isaacs. *The Art of Powerful Questions: Catalyzing Insight, Innovation, and Action*. Mill Valley, CA: Whole Systems Associated, 2003.

Acknowledgments

Thousands of people every year have trusted KLC with their aspirations for the future and dreams of having more impact with their leadership. Thank you for coming to programs in Wichita, inviting us into your companies, and logging in from your offices and dining rooms. We feel the energy of your commitment to do good work, grow your skills, and pass it forward. Each of you helped shape the ideas in this book.

Here are just a few who deserve special kudos.

We are grateful to our friends Marty Linsky and Ron Heifetz. This book builds on their powerful and disruptive ideas about leadership, like the distinction between adaptive challenges and technical problems and the productive zone of disequilibrium. We are among the thousands of leadership development professionals who link to Marty and Ron's work. Likewise, David Chrislip's fingerprints are on this book too. Our efforts to democratize the practice of leadership has its roots in David's work. Marty, Ron, and David are mentors and friends. The overly-used phrase "we are standing on the shoulders of giants" is apt here.

We are grateful to the Kansas Health Foundation. Steve Coen, who passed away as the manuscript was being finished, co-founded KLC and used his vision, authority and presence to help bring this one-of-a-kind idea to fruition. Steve's friendship and mentorship of Ed was especially important over the last 15 years. There would be no KLC without Steve. Marni Vliet Stone, you envisioned an organization that would build leadership capacity for the common good at a scale never before attempted. You exercised tremendous leadership to mobilize the Kansas Health Foundation to invest in such a bold dream. Jeff Usher, as our program officer, you have always been a partner, ready with wise advice, direct feedback and encouragement.

Ron Alexander, Patty Clark, Peter Cohen, Matt Jordan, Lynette Lacy, Shaun Rojas, and Chris Green each played a unique role in our first leadership development programs. You experimented and took risks to determine what we taught and how we taught it. You tested, innovated and documented. Shaun and Chris, it's a joy to have you at the helm as we seek to spread the impact of the KLC ideas through civic engagement and The Journal of the Kansas Leadership Center.

We are grateful to our board of directors and our audacious chair David Lindstrom for never hesitating to get into the productive zone. Thank you for supporting smart risks (like this book!) on behalf of a shared mission.

Edbert Abebe, Ron Carrerre, Bill Coy, Lisa Croxford, Ali Duvall, Marty Linsky, and Sarah Mali asked provocative questions about our book outline at just the right moment.

Tim Steffensmeier and Ahmadreza Shamsi Yousefi, we are grateful for answers to our research questions and for your constant curiosity about what more there is to learn about the activity of leadership.

Thank you, Amanda Cebula, for co-authoring *Your Leadership Edge*. Without that book we wouldn't have this book.

Every member of the KLC team has their DNA in this book. Staff, teachers, coaches, and civic facilitators, your work shines through the examples. Jamie Moeder managed the book-making process from inception to launch. Damon Young, you jumped right in. Darla Brunner, Maren Berblinger, Dennis Clary, Brittany Engle, Brianna Griffin, Ciara Huntly, Tyrena Judie, Carrie Lindeman, Ashley Longstaff, Idalia Loya, Clare McClaren, Julian Montes, Lucy Petroucheva, Shannon Pope, John Rolfe, Racquel Thiesen, Katy Weidner and DJ Whetter rose to the challenge of weaving book publishing into everything we do at KLC. Alejandro Arias, Jaryth Barten, Seth Bate, Kevin Bomhoff, Thane Chastain, Andy Huckaba, and Patrick Kelly gave invaluable feedback on an early (much, much longer) draft. Mary Banwart, Mildred Edwards, Dioane Gates, Anita Greenwood, Jill Hufnagel, Tina Khan, Brandon Kliewer, Tim Link, Joyce McEwen Crane, Adrion Roberson, Teresa Schwab, and Donna Wright, you and your teammates make these ideas come alive in virtual and in-person leadership development programs. Kaye Monk-Morgan, thank you for your stories of leadership moments in real life. Sam Smith, thank you for just-in-time edits and much more.

Todd Sattersten, publisher, editor, friend, it feels like we've known you forever. Thank you for responding to Ed's email and for getting so curious about this renegade group of Kansas rule-breakers. We never would have expected you to attend six days of virtual leadership programs, let alone get so excited about them!

Thank you, Joy Panos Stauber and Pat Byrnes for book design and illustrations that represent the high value we place on accessibility and inclusion. Pat, we know from experience with your cartoons in *Your Leadership Edge* that we'll find new meaning every time we put one of your drawings in front of an audience. Thank you, Claudia Amaro for making sure these ideas reach even more people with your translation of *When Everyone Leads* into Spanish.

Thank you to our private sector partners especially Vania Broderick-Dursun, Debbie Finch, Robin Hubar, Chris Huntley, Wanda Jones-Yeatman, Jonathan McRoy, Jeff Morris, D.J. Netz, Sheila O'Connor, Coleen Tabor, and René White. You have helped KLC become more responsive and entrepreneurial. Lori Alvarado you paved the way.

We appreciate our colleagues from leadership development institutions in places as far afield as Jerusalem, Abuja, Melbourne, New Orleans, and Baltimore. We love it that you have adopted our ideas and are using them in your own way. Shout out to Richard Dent, Cecile Garmon, Kathy Hallisey, Kristine Hilger, Jay Kaufman, Stephanie Molnar, Hugh O'Doherty, David Sachs, Lisa Croxford, and Valerie Stewart.

Thanks to all of the organizations that have partnered with KLC through Leadership Transformation Grants and Community Leadership Programs. Special thanks to Broderick Crawford, Irene Caballero, Rhonda Cott, Troy Leith, Jeanine McKenna, Lalo Muñoz, Mark Palen, Stacie Schmidt, Jeanette Siemens, Troy Unruh, Yazmin Wood, and Gary Wyatt. You challenge us to make the leadership framework ever more applicable to real life challenges.

Ashley Stanley, Charlotte, Peter and Claire, thank you for sharing Thomas with us. We miss him every day.

Julia wants to thank those who have my back and inspire me to do super-fun things like write *When Everyone Leads*, especially Bill McBride, Lake Harrier McBride, Donna and Jim Fabris, Marcia Reynolds, Tia Regier, Ronnie Brooks, Jan Davis, Laurene von Klan, and Davin Auble. And thank you, Alene Valkanas for challenging me to think big at a pivotal moment.

Ed wants to thank Joanna, Gabe, Jack, and Lizzie O'Malley. I love writing, but I love spending time with you more.

Ed and Julia are grateful to Mary Tolar for introducing us to one another.

A Bard Press book

Publisher: Todd Sattersten
Copyeditor: Rebecca Rider
Proofreading: Shannon Littlejohn
Text Design: Joy Panos Stauber, Stauber Brand Studio
Production and Ebook Layout: Happenstance Type-O-Rama
Jacket Design: Joy Panos Stauber, Stauber Brand Studio
Illustrations: Pat Byrnes

Many thanks to our early readers who provided valuable
comments and recommendations:
Phil Auxier , Tod Bolsinger, Amy Buckley, David Chrislip,
Lisa Croxford, Charlie Gilkey, Bobby Herrera, Jill Hufnagel,
Marty Linsky, Jonathan Long, Jeanine McKenna, Corey
Mohn, Lalo Muñoz, Sheila O'Connor, Patrick Rossol-Allison,
Lisa Perez-Miller, Sam Smith

When Everyone Leads: How The Toughest Problems Get Seen and Solved
Ed O'Malley and Julia Fabris McBride

Published by Bard Press, Portland Oregon

Bard Press
info@bardpress.com—www.bardpress.com

Ordering Information
For additional copies, contact your favorite bookstore or email
 info@bardpress.com. Quantity discounts are available.
Publisher's Cataloging-In-Publication Data
(Prepared by The Donohue Group, Inc.)

Names: O'Malley, Ed, 1975- author. | McBride, Julia Fabris, author.
Title: When everyone leads : how the toughest challenges are seen and solved /
      by Ed O'Malley & Julia Fabris McBride, Kansas Leadership Center.
Description: First edition. | Portland Oregon : Bard Press, 2022.
Identifiers: ISBN 9781885167903 (hardcover) | ISBN 9781885167958 (paperback) |
      ISBN 9781885167910 (ebook)
Subjects: LCSH: Leadership. | Management--Employee participation. | Problem solving.
Classification: LCC HD57.7 .O43 2022 (print) | LCC HD57.7 (ebook) | DDC 658.4092--dc23

First Edition: First Printing January 2023

When everyone leads,
we make progress on our most important challenges.